MARTHA MATILDA HARPER
AND THE AMERICAN DREAM

Writing American Women
Carol A. Kolmerten, *Series Editor*

Publicity photograph of Martha Matilda Harper.
Courtesy of Golden Memories.

MARTHA MATILDA HARPER

AND THE
American Dream

How One Woman Changed
the Face of Modern Business

JANE R. PLITT

SYRACUSE UNIVERSITY PRESS

This book is published with the assistance of a grant from the
John Ben Snow Foundation.

The paper used in this publication meets the minimum requirements of
American National Standard for Information Sciences—Permanence of
Paper for Printed Library Materials, ANSI Z39.48-1984.∞™

Library of Congress Cataloging-in-Publication Data
Plitt, Jane R.
Martha Matilda Harper and the American dream : how one woman changed the face of
modern business / Jane R. Plitt
p. cm. — (Writing American women)
Includes bibliographical references and index.
ISBN 0-8156-0638-9 (cloth : alk. paper)
1. Harper, Martha Matilda—Biography.   2. Businesswomen—United States—Biography.
3. Beauty shop supplies industry—Management.   I. Title.   II. Series.
HD9999.B253 U56 2000
338.7'68—dc21
[B]   99-085982

Manufactured in the United States of America

To Bess Rubin Plitt, my beloved grandmother,
who was my first entrepreneurial role model.
She demonstrated through words and deeds that women,
regardless of age, should be taken seriously

and to Jim Bruen, my treasured soul mate and husband,
who steadfastly encouraged me to heed my inner
voice and continuously provided the support of his
unconditional love with which to do it

Jane R. Plitt is a visiting scholar at the University of Rochester. As a business owner, labor arbitrator, and social justice advocate, Plitt has been recognized by the U.S. Small Business Administration as a Business Advocate and by SAVVY Magazine as one of fourteen outstanding women in New York State. She is also a proud retired soccer mom.

Contents

Illustrations

Acknowledgments

A PROJECT OF THIS MAGNITUDE, uncovering a buried story over six years, takes enormous good fortune and assistance. Fortuitously, I had all this and more from countless people who were there at critical moments, redirecting, encouraging, and providing technical assistance to me. Space constraints do not allow for personal recognition of all of these wonderful colleagues, friends, and family members. I am, however, indebted to them all.

Special recognition does need to be given to the cosmic forces that led me to the newspaper clipping about Martha Matilda Harper and ultimately to this story. There was also Robert Bantle, bank executive, whose love of history and community provided the corporate forum for me to uncover the story of Martha Matilda Harper.

Centa Sailer and Betty Wheeler, devoted Harper shop owners, shared their extraordinary hospitality, Harper connections, memories and skills, mementos, and photographs with me. Betty's now deceased husband, Warren, also deserves enormous thanks for his dedication, initiative, and perseverance in 1972 for saving and transporting boxes of Harper records with Betty's help; those documents were essential in understanding the Harper business and Martha's values. Many others in the Harper network (Harperites) gave me much time and critical information, among them Winifred Hines, Sally Knapp, Jim McGarvey, Hans Neumaier, Marie Personte, Jane Reed, Dorothy Ricker, Nancy Wise Smart, Martha Sweeney, Eunice Van Alystyne, Beryl Wickings, and Alice Wright. There were also delighted Harper customers and their families, including Helene Pancoast, Allyis D'Amanda, and Gene Van Voorhis, who shared their memories.

The Harper and MacBain* families welcomed me with open arms as I called, visited, and took away their treasured stories and letters. Each of them made me feel like an honorary member of the family. Of special note is Fausta Ahrens, Robert MacBain's ninety-year-old niece, who tenaciously saved and then shared her grandmother's, mother's, and uncle's correspondence with me. These letters provided precious insight. She also urged me to use them freely to tell the story honestly. Similarly, Jack and Robert Hoskinson provided me with their family's letters and stories, as did Douglas MacBain and his now deceased father, Robert, Esther MacBain Meeks, Merry MacBain Kruse, Bertha Hickey, Catherine O'Leary, Peggy Rettie, and Doreen Shosenberg.

The local newspapers, *Democrat & Chronicle, Rochester Business Journal,* and *Brighton Pittsford Post,* aided the treasure hunt by running stories about my search and enabling former Harper neighbors and friends, as well as Harperites and their family members, to connect with me. Those calls, clippings, and letters were essential stepping-stones.

My appointment as a visiting scholar at the University of Rochester was invaluable; particular thanks go to Nan Johnson and the Susan B. Anthony Center for making it possible. The University of Rochester's library staff gave caring help, particularly Karl Kabelac in the Rare Books division and Sally McMaster in the Interlibrary Loan division.

Community people also responded. John Hudak, owner of the former Harper headquarters, and Joanne Nulton, then owner of the former Harper mansion, enthusiastically opened their buildings to me. Cynthia Howk of the Landmark Society of Western New York documented the Harper home and laboratory. Linda Drummon provided access to the membership records of First Church of Christ, Scientist, and Anne E.

---

* For purposes of consistency, all MacBains are referred to in this book using this spelling, even though only some of the relatives followed this Scottish tradition.

Norris shared her spiritual insight into being both a Christian Scientist and an entrepreneur. Dr. Alice Rubenstein, psychologist/partner, Monroe Psychotherapy Center, freely gave her time and professional skill to help me better understand Martha and her emotional evolution. Jacqueline and Robert Sperandio, former business colleagues of mine, edited an early version of the book.

Dr. Mary Ellen Zuckerman, Professor of Marketing at the State University of New York at Geneseo, an absolute stranger, became a generous professional mentor. Terry Richman, Esq., connected me to the revealing will file of Luella Roberts. James Stewart, Esq., taught me how to use Surrogate Court records. The staff of the Monroe County Surrogate Court generously helped me locate and understand various court documents. The Monroe County Board of Elections opened its voting records to me. The Rochester Museum and Science Center and its staff warmly welcomed the opportunity to become the caring repository of all the Harper materials I discovered.

Historical agencies, including the Clarke Museum & Archives, the Charlotte-Genesee Lighthouse Historical Society, the Oakville Historical Society, and the Rochester Historical Society, shared their precious collections with me. Librarians at the New York Public Library, the Catherwood Library at the New York State School of Industrial and Labor Relations at Cornell University, the Library of Congress, and the Oakville Public Library provided valued support in finding fragments of the story. Simpson College shared its revealing MacBain files with me.

Karen Thure, a Harper essayist, graciously provided her records and encouragement. Dr. George Ritzer, Professor of Sociology at the University of Maryland, reviewed an early draft of my book. Dr. Carol A. Kolmerten, Professor of English at Hood College and editor of Syracuse University Press's Writing American Women series, gave critical early support to this story, which led to its publication, and her careful editing strengthened it.

Judy Columbus, Dr. Mimi Doi, Linda Joffe, and BJ Mann, devoted friends, tirelessly read, reread, coached, corrected, and supported me through multiple versions of the story. Sebby Wilson Jacobson and Steven Schaefer each urged me on at critical moments. Claire McGuire and Colleen McColgan provided invaluable assistance in proofing and indexing respectively.

Jim Bruen, my husband, and my children, Brett and Beth Plitt Bruen, patiently and lovingly endured the six-year journey of sharing me with Martha.

Finally, I am indebted to Martha Matilda Harper, who lived a life worth documenting and whose spirit will not die.

Introduction

I FIRST MET MARTHA MATILDA HARPER nearly fifty years after her death. She appeared to me in the form of an old newspaper clipping that I came across while researching a business project. Momentarily impressed with her accomplishments as a nineteenth-century businesswoman and captivated by her floor-length hair, I was more focused on completing my business assignment. After all, deadlines and deliverables were what kept my business going.

And yet, over the following months, I kept ruminating about her. Here was an early woman entrepreneur who created the first American retail franchise and was a pioneer in the beauty industry. Why had I not heard of her? Where was she recorded by history? And why had our first "encounter" created such a lasting—and intriguing—impression?

As I continued to focus on my growing business, my thoughts kept returning to the mysterious legacy of Martha Matilda Harper. How had an undereducated servant girl built an international franchise network of shops, complete with manufacturing and training centers, only for it to disappear into thin air? Why were Presidents, heads of state, and First Ladies her devoted customers? Naively I wondered how important she could be if the history books did not record her accomplishments. Then, more cynically, I asked who writes the history of such women.

After a year of such musing, my midlife curiosity pushed me over the edge. I decided to close my business and uncover Martha Matilda Harper's story, believing it would be a short, personal treasure hunt. I was to discover that the story would take six years to complete and was much larger than an individual portrait. In fact, Martha's story fit into a broader tapestry of women's business history, much of which remains only partially understood because, quite frankly, it is not known.

Digging into Martha Matilda Harper's past, I discovered a compelling if not disturbing trend: that certain lessons of history needed to be repeated simply because they were taught the first time by a woman. Over a hundred years ago, Martha Matilda Harper was a crusader for customer satisfaction and quality products and service. Her success was based on concepts that today determine business's cutting edge. She also believed in doing business ethically. As I discovered fragments of her life, I was astonished by how much she still has to teach us. Where might our country be today if we had built on Martha's business acumen, rather than having to re-create her vision?

It soon struck me that allowing Martha Matilda Harper's story to vanish was a metaphor for how undervalued women's lives have been in our society. In fact, its burial has hidden Martha's revolutionary attempt to change options for working-class women like herself. Her concept of retail franchising was not simply a brilliant business model, but a concrete means to offer ownership and female consciousness to her working-class sisters. She was redefining her own destiny and that of thousands of other women. Once I saw her journey in a broader context, my interest in this story grew.

Martha Matilda Harper's story is more than a triumphant personal life history. At some critical point, input from colleagues helped me connect her story to those of other innovative female entrepreneurs: dressmakers, milliners, beauty moguls, inventors, each of whom seized her limited opportunities and succeeded in her own way.

Success is such a personal benchmark. Martha's financial wealth was established simultaneously with raising the earning potential of thousands of her Harperites. She was not choosing to amass great wealth, but she was delighted to share it. Her new entrepreneurial scheme enlarged the economic pie of opportunity for the working-class segment of our country.

Blazing new paths for working-class women, Martha created the franchise system to share wealth at a time when the robber barons were destroying lives to enrich themselves. She wanted people to believe that if they were healthy, they were naturally beautiful. Her philosophy ran counter to the largely male-dominated beauty industry, which convinced women (and now men) that their beauty is dependent on their purchase of image-enhancing products.

Martha's life also reflected a society that arbitrarily limited opportunities by gender and class; even now, we still struggle to break down these artificial barriers. That she succeeded—in spite of being a servant for twenty-five years, and in the face of class- and gender-based obstacles—is compelling.

Martha's legacy is also written in the lives of the people she touched. It was revealing to discover that nearly fifty years after her death, men and women still revere her. She profoundly affected the lives of franchise owners, employees, and customers, and in that process, her story has stayed alive, waiting to be told. Having heard their voices, my mission was clear—to weave a living tale out of this veiled web of disjointed facts and memories, allowing a fuller appreciation of women's accomplishments in the past.

I learned that piecing a life together is different from writing a business plan with known assignments and deadlines. It requires patience, persistence, curiosity, an openness to discovering, not to mention interpreting nontraditional artifacts and a willingness to embrace the unknown. Numerous problems arose as I tried to uncover her story: the lack of historical citation, the challenge of finding living people who knew her, and contradictory memories, perspectives, and statements of facts. Like an archaeologist on a dig, I tried to unearth that which had long since been buried. I was fortunate to be welcomed into people's homes and worlds simply because I wanted to talk about their Martha.

Because so little of Martha's story was traditionally recorded, this biography blends recorded fact with treasured memories, letters, tangible remnants of business records, and the unwritten history found in walking the land where Martha and her family lived, experiencing the tradition-based Harper facial, or hearing the unspoken messages from Martha's and her husband's gravesites. Re-creating a life, especially the life of a woman who lived at a time when women's history was rarely valued, has been a major challenge. I made judgments about conflicting dates and stories based on the credibility of sources, consistency, and reasonableness. By example, although the *New York Times*'s obituary of Harper recorded her age as eighty-two, in fact she was ninety-three. I established her birth date from a tombstone and court testimony.

There was also something about Martha's life and work that touched me on an intensely personal level. Though separated by ninety years, each of us started her businesses at the age of thirty-one and was a champion of women's rights. Despite the passage of ninety years, each of us launched her enterprise at a time when women entrepreneurs were few and not highly regarded. Would Harper's business experiences have helped me and other business owners, male or female, in our quest for success? Could they still?

While I searched for details and practical payoff, it was Martha's soul that reverberated throughout the journey. It was her ability to maintain a humanity in her enterprise; to pioneer business practices and a franchise system that today dominates our retail economy; to think outside the box; to be consistent and principled; to persevere under circumstances most of us would have withered under; to make purposeful connections to both society's most prominent members and the more needy of our society, whose livelihoods and loyalties were inherently linked to the remarkable Martha Matilda Harper, that still captivate me.

MARTHA MATILDA HARPER
AND THE AMERICAN DREAM

Martha as successful entrepreneur, dressed for success.
Courtesy of Betty Wheeler.

CHAPTER ONE

Vanishing

WHEN MARTHA MATILDA HARPER DIED on August 3, 1950, she was famous. The American media recognized her as a female Horatio Alger. Among the obituaries included by her firm in the *Obituary Compilation Of Martha Matilda Harper,* one declared, "Too little, . . . has been said of women whose achievements have rivaled or outdone [men]. A book surely could be written about Martha Matilda Harper who built an international business" (*Obituary Compilation Of Martha Matilda Harper* 1950, 3).

Destined to be a poor nineteenth-century servant, Martha transformed her life into that of a successful businesswoman. She was not remembered for what she looked like—the woman with ravishing, floor-length chestnut hair—nor as the woman P. T. Barnum once tried to lure into his circus because of those phenomenal tresses. Instead, when Martha Matilda Harper died, it was her pioneering influence in the beauty industry that was recalled in the obituaries published in major newspapers throughout the country. This was highly unusual in the 1950s, when "women's stories" appeared on the society or women's page of newspapers. After her death, Martha's life was no longer a "woman's story"; she had achieved an equality with successful men.

Among the many obituaries compiled by the Harper business was a compelling statement by the *New York Times.* In its August 5, 1950, write-up, it called Harper: "one of the pioneers in the beauty business in the United States. . . . Susan B. Anthony, the pioneer suffragist, extolled Miss Harper's courage and initiative from many lecture platforms" (*Obituary Compilation Of Martha Matilda Harper* 1950, 3).

Hundreds of community leaders and Harper Shop owners and staff (Harperites) arrived in Rochester, New York, to pay homage. Their "Miss Harper" had died just as the annual Harper Reunion began. The Harper Method was a worldwide network of shops devoted to Martha's healthy approach to hair and skin care. At Harper Reunions, franchisees and their staffs were introduced to her new products and techniques while their skills were refreshed. In an interview, Centa Sailer, current owner of Martha's Harper Founder's Shop, recalled Martha's death and that memorable reunion this way: "We were there for the Reunion and we all went to the funeral parlor. She was larger than life even though she was physically small. Martha Matilda Harper was with you all the time" (1995).

Seven decades before Betty Friedan's *Feminine Mystique* encouraged women to embrace careers and break down sex-stereotyped boundaries, Martha Matilda Harper created a million-dollar business to provide economic choice for herself and other working-class women in a new field, the beauty industry. She seized opportunity, saved pennies, and with Scarlet O'Hara spunk she wrote a new tale for women. As recorded in the 1950 *Obituary Compilation Of Martha Matilda Harper,* the Associate Editor of the *Constitution,* Doris Lockerman, wrote:

> No respectable woman entered a beauty shop, nor would a respectable office building house one, when Martha Matilda Harper opened her first cosmetic business in Rochester, N.Y., using her own floor-length hair as advertisement.
>
> Miss Harper's death last week-end in the same city ended a success story that unfolded like a melodrama with a rags-to-riches plot, as one of the earliest cosmetic sagas. (2)

Truth be told, the newspapers got only half the story. In its obituary, the *New York Times* reported that Martha Matilda Harper was eighty-two years old. Martha was, in fact, ninety-three years old, but since she had married a much younger man, she misled people about her age.

The press also neglected to credit her with creating the first American business format (retail) franchise in the United States. (At its peak, there were over five hundred shops worldwide.) Nor did they explain why she was so bold and different. Dismissing the traditional capitalist approach of owner-take-all, Martha shared her profits with other women, particularly former servants like herself, in order to expand their life options; she believed that economic independence was the key to women's freedom. Her creativity, practicality, and principles were woven into her unique Harper franchise template.

Martha Matilda Harper tangibly changed women's lives. As Harper women described in their in-house newsletter, the *Harper Method Progress*, because of Martha they possessed economic security—money to travel, buy a car or a home, put their children and themselves through school, and the choice of whether to marry or not (*Harper Method Progress* 1926, 18). In that same newsletter, these women described their sense of pride that came with achievement and control. Marie Johnson experienced a new joy when she became the Carmel, California, Harper Shop owner. She said she felt "terribly important! It's a grand and glorious feeling" (*Harper Method Progress* 1926, 76).

Martha Matilda Harper, a little woman who stood less than five feet tall, gave her "girls" a feeling of hope and choice. She empowered them to take responsibility for themselves and their lives. She gave them a career, self-confidence, and a profession.

While Martha took on society's mores and the power establishment, even breaking Victorian tradition by rejecting society's preassigned roles for women, her persona was that of the ultimate lady. Though widely known for her gentle and kind nature, Martha, unlike most women of her day, stated quite clearly what she was doing and why. Forthrightly, in the *Harper Method Textbook*, required reading for all her "girls," she spoke about how consciously she built a worldwide business empire "brick by brick, woman by woman" (1926, 3). Martha knew exactly how bold her feat was, and in that textbook she shared her vision and pride with them.

Long after Martha's death in 1950, her business continued. In the 1960s, according to former Harperite Betty Wheeler, Jacqueline Kennedy had Harper Method treatments in the White House, and a May 22, 1968, White House check from Lady Bird Johnson to a Connecticut Harper shop indicates that she and Mrs. Laurance Rockefeller enjoyed such treatments, too. In the 1990s, many women, like Mrs. (Helen) Lee Shaffer and Alpha Jones, still valued their former Harper Shop affiliation. Shaffer's Reading, Pennsylvania, newspaper announcement of her fiftieth wedding anniversary, (March 7, 1993) proudly recalled that she was a retired Harper Shop owner. An obituary in the August 12, 1996, *State Journal Register* (Springfield, Ill.) highlighted Jones's achievement— owning a Harper Shop for more than forty years.

To be a Harperite was a significant life experience that Sally Knapp, of the Baltimore area, described during an interview as "a life-giving opportunity with career options I never would have had and social connections that made us feel like family" (Knapp 1997). At age eighty- three, Jane Reed, Harper Shop owner in Florida, continues to serve customers including the great-granddaughter of Dr. Alexander Graham Bell. During an interview with Jane Reed, she explained, "It is my life" (Reed 1997). The lives of those women and thousands of others were fundamentally altered by Martha Matilda Harper.

Martha was a consistent, appealing person, at work and at home, who revolutionized the American way of doing business, women's right to control their economic fate, and our image of beauty. Following her deep commitment to Christian Science, she integrated her spiritual be- liefs into her day-to-day supportive demeanor. Honor, fair play, whole- some respect for others, honesty, and her faith in God were unwavering principles that governed her daily behavior.

Martha treated people kindly. As Esther MacBain Meeks, a niece who lived with her during the 1940s, recalled in an interview, "She was genuinely nice, living her Christian Science faith" (1997). Now in her eighties, Meeks poignantly recalled when Martha visited her family in Iowa and gave her 75 cents. With Martha's money, Meeks promptly bought jewelry from the five-and-ten-cent store; her parents insisted that she return it. Seeing her pain, Martha instantly took off her neck- lace and placed it around her niece's neck (1996c). Caring, sensitive, and willing to share with children, family, friends, and her Harperites—that was Martha.

Mysteriously, as if caught in an information warp between Harper customers and owners and the rest of the American public, Martha Matilda Harper's story vanished after her death. Its fate was not unlike other women's entrepreneurial accomplishments. As a woman and wife of a plantation owner, Catherine Littlefield Green in 1794 shared her idea for separating cotton with guest Eli Whitney. He is remembered as the inventor of the cotton gin, and she is not. According to Martha Louise Rayne, author of *What Can a Woman Do*, a nineteenth-century book on women's careers:

> The spherical shape of the bullet is the result of a woman's experimenting. . . . Miss Louise McLaughlin . . . invented a method of under-glaze upon pottery, and desiring that all artists should share its benefits, explained her process to everyone who asked. . . . Mrs. Ann Harned Manning in 1817–1818 perfected [a reaping and mowing machine] which was patented by her husband. . . . [Other women invented] the baby carriage, [the] deep-sea telescope, [was invented] by Mrs. Mather and improved by her daughter, for bringing the bottoms of ships into view without raising them in dry-dock, . . . inspecting wrecks, . . . examining for torpedoes. (1884, 115–17)

Those were real nineteenth-century inventions, but the inventors' names and gender were forgotten.

In Martha's case, she was once famous. What happened?

CHAPTER TWO

Uncovering Martha's Roots

MARTHA MATILDA HARPER was born in 1857 in Munn's Corner, a shadow of a village on the outskirts of prosperous Oakville, Ontario. Being the daughter of Robert Harper was trouble enough, but she was also born poor and female. For most ordinary people, this unenviable circumstance would have been an insurmountable life sentence. But Martha, a willful young girl, was not ordinary, and neither was her life.

The hardships she faced were fundamental. Because of Canada's class and gender structure, Martha's life was subject to male domination and decision-making. Her livelihood was tied to a family economy where the money generated was dependent on household activity. In many mid-nineteenth-century households, men dominated these sites of production. As a result, women's personal and productive lives were often determined by their husbands, fathers, or brothers, who controlled both the household and the means of production.

In such an environment, Martha could see her future reflected in her mother, Beady, sad-faced and thin, her dark hair pulled back in a severe bun. Beady's hair symbolized her life: controlled, one-dimensional, and tightly pulled into its proper place. Beady Gifford Harper's accomplishments were similar to those of other poor rural women; she married, gave birth, and died. Little more is known about her, other than that she was Robert's third wife; the first two having died of complications in childbirth. The most fertile of the wives, Beady died at the age of fifty-one on June 11, 1885, after bearing ten children.

Martha as a child. *Courtesy of* Golden Memories.

Martha was born on September 10, 1857, the fourth child, preceded by two sisters, Sarah and Elizabeth, and a brother, Ephriam. Like all her siblings, according to Martha's corporate memoir, *Golden Memories*, she arrived without fanfare, destined to be a burden (1938, 2). Martha's insistent personality emphasized her painful presence. The crude reality was that she was one more mouth to feed, one more body to clothe. Two siblings born later, Nellie and James, died in infancy. For the Harper family, life and death were part of a harsh natural rhythm.

Not far from the giant oak forests surrounding the Harpers' one-room cabin, life was different for others. By chance of birth, Martha was an impoverished Harper; other local women, born into wealth, faced different challenges of societal constraint. Hazel Matthews, author of

Martha's mother, Beady Harper, and her sister Emma.
Years later Martha sent Emma to Europe for musical training.
Courtesy of Golden Memories.

the authoritative history of Oakville, described the pampered experience
of a local upper-class bride at the time. "The bride, who is often a young
girl from sixteen to twenty years of age, is doomed for [a week] to sit
upon a sofa, or recline in an easy-chair dressed in the most expensive

manner, to receive her guests. Well she knows that herself, her dress, the furniture of her room, even her cake and wine, will undergo the most minute scrutiny, and be the theme of conversation among all the gossips of the place for the next nine days" (Matthews 1953, 230). Such was the gentler, but still confining, world of upper-class Oakville women.

Martha's life in Munn's Corners stood apart, like a poor relative. Her village, just a few miles north of Oakville, offered a much humbler world, with each day's survival being an accomplishment. From a distance Martha spied the Georgian brick homes and businesses of Oakville, a bustling port. As Martha later recorded in *Golden Memories,* "Hidden from the passerby, back on its outskirts, Oakville ignores many a different home of a different sort, where hardship and privation are the rule" (1938, 1).

In 1857, the year that Martha was born, Oakville became an incorporated town with a population of one thousand. With the recent advent of a rail system and ports linking Toronto and Hamilton to Oakville, the village changed from an industrial hub to a recreational center, a convenient retreat for wealthy Toronto and Hamilton residents (Matthews 1953, 222). Oakville also had a thriving community elite, many of whom were relatives of its white founder, William Chisholm.

In her local history of the area, Matthews noted that the Mississauga Indians originally inhabited the area and occupied the banks of Sixteen Mile Creek. In fact, in 1827, that 960 acres, known as the Reserve of the Sixteen, was sold, for $4.25 an acre, to the enterprising William Chisholm, an established storekeeper, banker, public leader, and shipowner. Envisioning a dramatically expanded community, he saw the commercial potential of this area and realized its growth could be fueled by traffic generated from a port on the northern shore of Lake Ontario, and fed by Sixteen Mile Creek (Matthews 1953, 5–12). With money, determination, business savvy, and political connections, he successfully planned and created the Oakville community, and by 1833 his dream had come true. He and his heirs prospered, playing a leading role in the affairs of the community.

Martha's father, Robert, wanted such wealth and success. His problem was that he did not want to work for it. As a child, Martha was

Robert Harper, Martha's father,
who valued his image more
than his family duties.
Courtesy of the Harper family.

dependent on her father—an irresponsible man, consumed with himself
and his woeful laziness. Robert had a reputation as a dreamer, not a
doer. He preferred to fantasize himself a gentleman, riding to the hounds
like his English ancestors, rather than earning his living by tailoring
(Thure 1976, 94). Robert was lured into believing he could become a
rich landowner by a local teacher, Arthur Cole Verner, who also wanted
to join the affluent of the area.

Verner served as master of the Oakville Common School in the 1840s
and 1850s. Matthews postulated that when Verner saw the amount of farm
produce moving from the north, passing along the 7th Line Plank Road,
to Oakville Harbor, the idea grew of a planned community near Oakville
with a church, a school, and even an English village green. He hoped that
his new community, Vernerville, three-quarters of a mile north of Oakville,
would attract people and make him wealthy (Matthews 1953, 195–96).

Martha's father was a perfect candidate for investing in Vernerville.
With the help of an innovative mortgage scheme, small farmers and

The Vernerville cabin where Martha grew up. *Courtesy of* Golden Memories.

tradesmen like Harper had an opportunity to purchase their land on time. In November 1862, Robert bought 4.5 acres in the southwest corner of Verner's community for $170. On that land may have been the Lyon's Cabin, presently on display in the Oakville community; on the basis of the local Hawley Records, it may have once been the Harpers' home. This one-room home of hand-hewn logs was dark, simple, confining, even depressing; but to Robert it held promise. As it turned out, neither Vernerville nor Robert was ever successful.

A tailor by trade, Robert listed his profession as "gentleman" on the deed of sale for his Vernerville plot (Hawley Records). Such an overstatement was not a momentary lapse of honesty. In fact, it signaled his discomfort with who he really was. Ultimately, that discomfort led to a spiraling lack of responsibility and honesty that would soon traumatize Martha's life.

Robert lacked character. Martha, always one to find good things to say about anyone, described her father as "stern, unflinching English pioneer . . . too pre-occupied with his daily struggle to pay much heed to . . . [her]" (*Golden Memories* 1938, 2). The truth was that Robert was selfish and fickle, unable to face reality or his responsibilities. He could not reconcile his English family's well-to-do past with his pressing financial burdens.

Two years after Robert began paying off his Vernerville plot, he faced a major financial crisis and made a fateful decision to abandon his fatherly responsibilities. Choosing to hold onto his land, he bound out seven-year-old Martha to bring in extra money for the family. She was simply sent away, far from her family—particularly her mother, who gave her whatever love and security she had known. So ended Martha's childhood, as eventually it ended for all of her siblings. According to Catherine O'Leary, Martha's grandniece, her Great-Grandfather Robert gave away all of his children (1996b).

Years later, Martha reflected on her mother's inability to keep her family together. In *Golden Memories,* Martha used a phrase that described her mother's helplessness: "Beaten at last in her heroic battle for her children" (1938, 2). Her words suggest that Martha saw her mother as a powerless victim, just as she was. Her servitude and her mother's defeat were her father's doing.

Although known for her kind and Christian ways, Martha eventually got even. Twenty years after her business was launched, she erected a sizable tombstone in the Oakville Cemetery, Centre Lot #59, for her mother and her two infant siblings. Her father received no such tribute; in fact, no record has been found of his burial. Martha Matilda Harper appeared to have cut him out of her life, just as he cut her out of his.

Meanwhile, seven-year-old Martha was taken to the community of Leskard, to become a servant. It was a village more than sixty miles east of Oakville. Situated on three streams, by the mid-1850s Leskard was bustling with milling and farm activity, and had a growing population of 250 people. Soon it would become a village and call itself Rochester. (Ironically, Martha eventually moved to Rochester, New York where she made her fortune.) However, in 1856, the community's name was changed to Leskard, because another Ontario community had already claimed the name Rochester.

By the time Martha arrived in Leskard, she was among strangers. She was introduced to the people she was to serve. John Gifford, her mother's brother, was a huge man who, according to family records, weighed over three hundred pounds. Then she met John's wife, Elsie Maria, and her two spinster aunts, Roby Ann and Rannie. Martha was to attend to their demands. Her grandmother, Thursay Pickle, who lived in the area until 1873, was true to her name; she looked like a sour pickle (Hickey 1996).

Martha's head must have swirled with bewilderment. This was not a warm extended family outreach. Instead, Martha committed to a serious business proposition. She was expected to earn her keep. As a young child in Munn's Corner and Vernerville, life had been hard for her, full of exhausting tasks, but buffered by her mother; in Leskard, life would prove heartless. Her three strict aunts demanded service and provided little love. When Martha reflected on her life and its various struggles in a June 6, 1914, interview with Marjory MacMurchy, a writer for *The Toronto,* she commented that it was only during her childhood that she really endured hardships (1914, 21); then she was alone and dependent on others.

According to Canadian historian Marjorie Griffin-Cohen, it was highly unusual for a girl Martha's age to be put into service; in the nineteenth century, Canadian teenage girls often engaged in such work before marriage (1988, 85–86). Domestic service was one of the few work options available to these poor girls. While men's wages rose in the early 1850s, female servant wages changed little, reflecting the lack of earning alternatives available to women. In all likelihood, Martha made less than three or four dollars a month.

Expectations for her were clear. In their history of nineteenth-century Ontario women, Acton, Goldsmith, and Shepard concluded that "A good servant was clean, celibate, obedient, respectable, hardworking, and an early riser" (1974, 83). In Canada, general servants were in great demand. There was never an end to Martha's tasks—cooking, cleaning, sewing, and taking care of the house and farm.

Martha's lost childhood fundamentally altered her. It changed more than her location. Roles reversed, and Martha became the caretaker of her family. To help her parents survive, according to *Golden Memories,* she sent them all of her meager earnings (1938, 2). Despite, or because of, her abandonment, Martha, though young, believed she had to make things right and that she was the family glue. Later, when she built her business, she assumed the role of responsible and powerful mother, becoming almost a Mother Superior. In her letters to Harper staff, known as Harperites, she referred to them as "My dear girls."

Psychologist Dr. Alice Rubenstein suggested that Martha's success at surviving her childhood trauma created her backbone; Martha learned she could avoid emotional vulnerability by relying only on herself. Her abandonment resulted in her gaining an inner strength that she tried to pass on to her "children," the Harper Shop owners (Rubenstein 1997b). Years later, a Harper Shop owner from Harrisburg, Pennsylvania, recalled in the *Harper Method Progress* that part of the Harper training included a discussion about Martha's motto: "Be equal to any problem that arises. Never give up. Be the master" (1926, 9).

Faced with forced servitude, Martha learned how to make it, alone, in spite of her seemingly powerless condition. Bright, quick-minded, and physically adept, she did what she had to do. She mastered the ability to read people: Would they be kind or cruel? Could they be trusted or not? She learned the art of pleasing others, fulfilling their needs, and managing her needs on her own. She was, after all, a servant. Submissiveness was the unwritten code for domestics. Passivity and deference became her mask, but underneath was a rebellious mind desperately searching for a way to end her misery. Though her childhood had been destroyed, she persisted in dreaming about a different life.

Such a dream was unrealistic. Martha should have assumed she would marry, like her mother, and like the overwhelming majority (86 percent) of Ontario women in their thirties who in 1851 were wives (based on the data compiled by historian Griffin-Cohen [1988, Appendix 165]). Yet Martha perceptively understood that marriage would more than likely put her husband in charge of her future.

Even though there was legislative progress for women in the mid-1800s, their options were still limited. Prior to 1859, there was little legal protection for married women in English Canada because of the English common law premise that in marriage a woman and man were one and the one was the man. In 1855 an act was passed in Ontario that gave women the possibility of obtaining custody of their children under twelve years of age, with the caveat that it would occur only "as the judge saw fit" (Griffin-Cohen 1988, 46). Further, Griffin-Cohen documents that in 1859, when Ontario women won the right to own property they had held before marriage, there were many hitches. For instance, the property had to have clearly been in their name. Simply put, a wife still "belonged to her husband and while the law legally entitled her to make a will, her heirs could only be her husband or her children" (Griffin-Cohen 1988, 47).

In 1872, married women in Ontario were allowed to keep their own earnings. However, the law excluded a wife's earnings where her husband had a fiscal interest, such as work in a family farm. In addition, the wife needed permission to work outside the home for wages or in her own business.

Choice, then, was not a part of most Ontario women's lives, and especially not part of Martha's early life. In general, there were only limited opportunities for all Canadian women, and even fewer for poor ones. In 1881, there was one female servant for every 16.2 Canadian households. For poor Ontario women, servitude was a dismal way of life, as documented by Acton, Goldsmith and Shepard: "long hours of work, lack of freedom, and lack of privacy must have made domestic service seem like a kind of modern-day slavery. . . . Servants . . . had very little time off; except for one afternoon a week and the occasional Sunday. The domestic servant was tied to her workplace and her employer's supervision twenty-four hours a day" (1974, 57).

Living in their employers' homes, servants had little privacy, dignity, and control over their lives. Martha worked from dawn to dusk. At night she probably retreated exhausted to her snug sleeping area, where she brushed her locks to calm herself. She wrote in *Golden Memories* that she latched onto a friend's prediction that "some day your hair would make your fortune" (1938, 3). Likely she thought of herself as a Rapunzel, abused, exhausted, imprisoned, ready to be freed. Over the years, when no one rescued her, perhaps Martha realized that only she and her beautiful hair had remained steadfast. Her locks, thick, chestnut-colored, and long, became almost a banner of presence. They declared, *I exist. Notice me.*

Likely Martha came to recognize just how invisible women were in her new world. While she labored, it was men's lives that seemed to matter, to be recorded in local newspapers and history books. Few specifics can be found about Martha while she worked in Leskard. What we know about her life is simply the reality thousands of other girls experienced as general household servants. We can also glean details from what was recorded about her Uncle John, a powerful community force.

Local township records compiled by John Squair reveal that besides owning a farm on poor land, John Gifford had a clover mill and a grain elevator. In addition, he conducted auctions (Squair 1927, 508, 561). He was an energetic worker, doing what he had to do to generate a living. In sharp contrast to her father, Uncle John worked hard and seized opportunities.

During these years, Martha likely observed entrepreneurship in action. Watching her uncle, she saw how hard he worked, and how he reaped the profits from his efforts. In contrast, she saw herself working hard, too; she lugged water, swept floors, and washed clothes. Her payoff was room and board and meager earnings that went to her parents. There was little hope that on a servant's wages she could ever accumulate wealth. Slowly, Martha Matilda Harper came to understand that servitude was a doomed female destiny. She would spend almost twenty-five years trying to change it.

As reported in Leetooze's township history, her Uncle John must have been a showman. The history recalled early newspaper coverage that stated, "Leskard is not as lively as it used to be when the late John Gifford was 'head toot' in the Orange Society and wore a long red cloak, on the glorious twelf [sic] [commemorating the defeat of the Irish Catholics at the Battle of the Boyne], that the boys all admired. Those were the days when Leskard took her turn having the annual Orange celebration" (Leetooze 1988, 151).

Township records report that Gifford displayed regalia everywhere, even at temperance meetings. He was a passionate man who publicly celebrated the defeat of the Irish Catholics and his strong abhorrence of drink. What these records also reveal is Gifford's inclination to join with others for a cause he believed in. The idea of creating a network of people who shared a common bond of beliefs seemed both alien and intriguing to Martha. As an isolated servant, the thought of a family of believers must have warmed her, as must her uncle's underlying belief in women's rights and his demonstration of the power of business. While her Uncle John was often outlandish, dressed in his costumes, he was bold and a believer in causes. While his clownish antics were not a behavior pattern Martha would mimic, his passion about women's rights surely captivated her. These were radical ideas that needed time and opportunity to fully gestate within Martha.

Some time after the age of twelve, Martha went to work for a physician who would alter her life. Although we know this occurred through a December 6, 1948, letter written by Martha's husband, Robert MacBain, we lack the name of the physician. Evidence suggests it was Dr. Weston Leroy Herriman, son of the township's first resident doctor, Dr. Luther Herriman.

Though cultured and respected, the Herrimans were outsiders. Dr. Luther Herriman's background almost prevented him from becoming a physician. Because he refused to take the loyalty oath to England, he was initially unable to graduate from medical school. Later, he won his appeal because of the need to establish a medical faculty in 1854. In exchange for entering the first class of medical instructors, Herriman was allowed to graduate. He returned with a medical degree in hand to Orono, a neighboring village larger than Leskard, with nearly eight hundred people (Squair 1927, 76, 239).

When Herriman established his Orono practice, two other doctors also opened their practices in the area. Given such competition, on April 9, 1857, Herriman placed an advertisement in the *Orono Star,* the local paper, announcing that he sold drugs and medicines. Unlike those of his competitors, his ad distinctly mentioned that he sold fine hairbrushes and toothbrushes. This suggests his interest in hair care, which became the powerful bond between Martha and him.

Dr. Herriman, an idealist, left Orono in the 1860s to serve the North in the American Civil War; the casualties of that war painfully taught him new surgery skills. After his war service, he returned to Orono, where he reopened his practice and married. When his first wife died suddenly, he needed someone to take care of his household.

Since Dr. Herriman had been initiated as a member of the Sons of Temperance before October 21, 1856, Martha's Uncle John and he likely were acquaintances, if not friends. Herriman may have asked Gifford about Martha's availability. We know that soon after Herriman's wife's death, he left Orono for nearby Port Hope. It is likely that Martha went with him as his housekeeper. Later, he remarried and remained in Port Hope until 1881.

Though the Herriman connection is the result of deduction, we do know that the doctor for whom Martha worked was a wonderful teacher and likely a cultured man with strong European roots. Harper essayist Karen Thure suggests that through exposure to the doctor's family, Martha may have acquired the air of refinement and poise later attributed to her (1976, 94).

This doctor patiently instructed her about the physiology of hair and its growth needs. Martha probably practiced on the women in the doctor's family as part of her duty as a household servant. Through instruction and practice, she learned the importance of brushing and stimulating the scalp's blood flow. The doctor also taught her about scalp hygiene, a revolutionary concept about keeping hair clean at a time when lack of good soap and hot water encouraged infrequent hair washings. From the doctor Martha learned to respect scientific principles, a precept she would uphold for her entire life.

The more Martha asked, the more the doctor shared his knowledge of anatomy, especially as it affected hair conditions (Thure 1976, 94). He was also a herbalist who possessed a secret-formula tonic, which made hair and scalp healthier and more beautiful. The doctor taught Martha that, "keeping your hair always clean is the first essential step to hair beauty. . . . To do that, you must brush well with castile suds, and rub this herbal tonic vigorously into the scalp, then rinse with warm water" (Maas 1979, 6).

With the tonic's use, Martha's thick mane grew longer; in fact, it graced the floor when she untied it. Her hair continued to be her banner of distinction; unfurled, it not so subtly proclaimed *I am different*.

In various published accounts of her life, Martha stated that she was given a secret hair tonic formula by a physician of Germanic heritage as he lay on his deathbed. While certainly that story created a dramatic image, its veracity is uncertain. Possibly she exaggerated, having gotten the formula from Dr. Herriman as a parting gift when he left the area for Lindsay, Ontario. Or possibly it was Dr. Herriman's father's formula, which he may have shared with his son and then with Martha. The elder Dr. Herriman died in 1879.

We do know that Martha Matilda Harper obtained a hair tonic formula and understood its importance. She recognized its potential and began to strategize how it might change her life.

At about the same time, Martha received an unidentified letter that helped her locate her future home. As recalled in *Golden Memories,* "It painted a picture of a land of promise, of action and opportunity. . . . The letter was from Rochester, NY and while she knew only that it was vaguely across the lake, it became her Mecca from that day on" (1938, 4).

In 1882, Monroe County Surrogate Court Records indicate, at the age of twenty-five, Martha Matilda Harper redirected her life (M. Harper 1933). She set her sights southward to a new country, holding a knotted handkerchief with sixty hard-earned silver dollars and the formula wrapped inside. She also carried a brown ceramic jug full of that potent hair tonic; that jug would come to symbolize the roots of her independence (Huntington 1946, 4; Thure 1976, 94). In Oakville, Orono, Leskard, and Port Hope, Martha was labeled, bound by her family, class, and gender. She could change none of this.

As Lake Ontario's waters crashed on the Canadian shore, Martha Matilda Harper could look across to Rochester, New York, and see hope. Determined, with little to lose, she fled Canada.

CHAPTER THREE

Choosing Rochester and Christian Science

MARTHA SAW A COMPELLING ROUTE AHEAD. She was traveling south, across Lake Ontario, which to the Iroquois, the area's early settlers, meant Lake Beautiful. This lake would connect Martha to a new country, just as the Erie Canal was bringing thousands of other immigrants west to seek their fortune. Many, like Martha, stayed in Rochester and shared their skills and vision with the community.

Getting to Rochester was the challenge. While boarding the steamship *Norseman,* with its enormous wheel, was momentous for Martha, it would be an ordinary voyage for the ship, which daily made the border crossing. The *Norseman* steamed out of its Canadian berth, crossed Lake Ontario, and arrived before noon at the Port of the Genesee. Traveling at ten knots, the ship connected two countries as if they were intimate friends swapping stories. As interviews with Genesee Lighthouse Historic Society members revealed, the seventy-mile journey across the lake was made by people and by products to be traded, either Rochester-area goods such as cherries, apples, and milled grain, or Canadian exports like lumber and fish. Sometimes the hold overflowed with products, which, along with animals, were loaded onto the deck with the passengers (Roemer 1997; Girvin 1997). They produced a cacophony of sound and smell, slightly jarring but full of life.

Martha Matilda Harper had a one-way ticket to her American refuge. As the ship edged forward, she glimpsed the Port of the Genesee, gateway to Charlotte, an incorporated village since 1869, which bordered the city of Rochester. With nearly ninety thousand people in 1880, Rochester was the twenty-second largest city in America. In such a city, Martha hoped to find her pot of gold.

Three lights beamed out at her, one from each pier and one from the stone lighthouse built in 1822. Their beams invited her onward, into the northerly flowing Genesee River, where the boats docked just north of the lighthouse, near the fruit warehouse and the train station. The docks were conveniently located for easy transport of people and products. Before anyone departed, the Harbor Master climbed on board the steamship, dutifully checking passengers (Spelman, *Spelman's Notebook* n.d.).

Following procedure, Martha and the other passengers debarked. The boat turned around on the east side of the river, in the process perhaps inadvertently catching the lines of people fishing with spoons. As she hurried toward her new home, Martha likely saw people stopping to visit the taverns that dotted Charlotte's River Street.

Martha, however, had other priorities. She was banking on Rochester to transform her status and reality. She was still a poor woman. She had left Canada a servant, and she came to Rochester also as a domestic. Her profession had not changed, only her location.

Serious, observant, and anxious for a new start, Martha needed time to cast off her servitude. Meanwhile, she carried her prized bundles to her new home. Whether she had previously arranged to work for the prominent attorney Luther Hovey and his wife, Leah Charlotte, we do not know. However, in 1882 she became the Hoveys' household maid and worked in their mansion at 881 East Main (Harper 1933, 205).

Martha entered the Hovey home, a stately two-story Victorian structure, complete with shutters and glassed-in cupola, and was promptly introduced to her new surroundings and role. As the housemaid, she served her employers and their friends. The Hoveys' life effervesced with optimism, while her future remained on hold, secreted away in her jug of tonic. Her current job was that of devoted servant. In that role she bided her time and listened, learning about the community where she hoped to change her prospects.

From conversations she overheard at the Hoveys, Martha likely learned about the "jewel of downtown"—the Powers Building—where the

Martha when she first came to Rochester.
Courtesy of Golden Memories.

affluent of Rochester shopped and transacted their business. Mr. Hovey's law office was there. The Powers Building, a "fire-proof" building with an ornate cast-iron facade, was the showpiece of downtown, located at the center of the city's commercial activity. It housed banks, law offices, shops, and an art gallery showcasing building owner Daniel Powers's personal collection of over one thousand works of art, including a breathtaking room of sculpture. At the urging of concerned women, an exchange where artists could display and sell their work was opened in 1882.

The building literally kept growing, with more floors and mansard roofs added, as Powers successfully engaged in a competition to erect the tallest structure in Rochester. The Powers Building was where Rochester's action was.

Privately, Martha made plans to have her business connected to that wonderful structure. She believed that if she was to be successful, her business needed to be associated with the rich and powerful. They could afford her services and products, and they had the class and connections to expand the demand for them.

Certainly, Daniel Powers was a key force; he was among the area's richest, and he owned the community's center of attraction. Martha noted with enthusiasm that he was a self-made businessman. Orphaned at an early age, he made his way to Rochester and became quite successful. Local Rochester history books report that he became a wealthy private banker by investing in the Union during the Civil War. Since the North won, he prospered.

Powers also married well—very well, according to Elizabeth G. Holahan, President of the Rochester Historical Society. Society gossip suggested that was how he really became rich. While Martha understood the impressiveness of how he had transformed his life, she knew their paths toward success would differ. As a woman, she believed marriage would not improve her career opportunities, as it may have done for Powers; instead, marriage would likely diminish her opportunities. Her steps to success would therefore have a slower pace than his. She needed to work hard, save what she could, learn by observing, and certainly not marry—at least not until she established herself.

Yet Martha, like many in the community, found encouragement in Powers's rags-to-riches story. In 1871 he had invested over $392,000 to complete the first phase of his building, enduring the heckling of the community when he tore down the popular Eagle Tavern to build it. In fact, when the project began in 1868, the building was called "Powers Folly." Once the first phase of the building was finished, Powers was

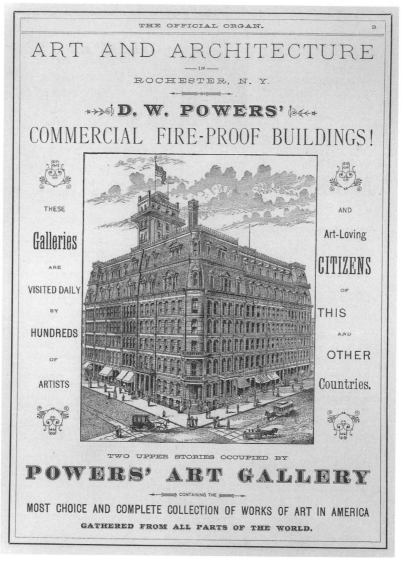

Powers Building, from an advertisement for the Powers Art Gallery, which opened in 1875 with a 25¢ admission fee. At its height of popularity, forty thousand people annually visited the thirty-room gallery. *Courtesy of the First National Bank.*

redeemed in the public eye (*First National Bank Celebration* 1994, 3–5). That Powers had triumphed in this community encouraged Martha to believe that she could, too.

Martha likely was also heartened to learn how the community of Rochester began in 1803, when Colonel Nathaniel Rochester and his partners purchased swampland in upstate New York. After surveying parts of it, in 1810, at the age of fifty-eight, Rochester, like Martha, left his comfortable world in Hagerstown, Maryland; giving it up to live in a free state, he came north to raise his family of twelve children and to free his slaves (Merrill 1986, 26–27). Ultimately, he shared both his name and his ideals of equality with the area.

Such stories probably took on almost legendary proportion for Martha; to her the community was full of visionary individuals. No one person determined Rochester's character or entrepreneurial complexion. By 1850, many of Rochester's early leaders had either gone further west or had died, including Colonel Rochester, who died in 1831. More newcomers, like herself, had come, and held other visions, especially in terms of business. Many brought their Old World skills to Rochester, as well as a fundamental belief that the status quo could be challenged.

Entrepreneurial know-how and creativity percolated both below and above the city's surface. Rochester historian Blake McKelvey documented the inventiveness of Rochesterians—Josephus Requa was called the father of the machine gun, which was used at the end of the Civil War. In 1852 the first application of a machine to sew shoes occurred in Rochester (McKelvey 1941, 13). Another Rochester historian, Arch Merrill, highlighted other Rochester inventions. In 1877 George Selden created the first internal-combustion engine and the prototype of the gas-run car. Architect James Cutler stirred the community when in 1883 he designed and installed the still used Cutler mail chute, allowing for easy collection of mail from upper floors of tall buildings (Merrill 1986, 90–92). Rochester seemed to be a home of innovation.

The more Martha Matilda Harper heard, the more she felt she belonged in Rochester. With its history of incorporating new ideas, spawning new businesses like Western Union and Bausch & Lomb, it was a perfect place to launch her business scheme.

The community was also full of suffragists. From them, Martha learned that the seeds for the area's support of women's rights had been planted as far back as the Seneca Indians, the first inhabitants of this city by the lake. Recently the community had been abuzz with Susan B. Anthony's and others' efforts to help women achieve their political and social rights.

A well-educated Quaker, Anthony had become a well-known women's rights advocate based in Rochester. She had caused quite a ruckus in 1872 when she declared that nothing prohibited women from voting. She "told delegates [attending] the suffrage convention to go home and vote" (Anthony 1975, 277). Along with fifty other Rochester-based women, Anthony promptly tried to register to vote on November 1, 1872; ultimately she and fifteen other women voted (Anthony 1975, 278–79). Singled out as the test case, Anthony was arrested; her trial was moved to Canandaigua, where Judge Ward Hunt presided. According to the proceedings of the case, published by the *Rochester Democrat & Chronicle,* the judge directed the jury to find her guilty, and they did ("An Account of the Proceedings of the Susan B. Anthony Trial" 1874, 3). While Anthony lost her case, she became a cause célèbre and refused to pay the fine. Afraid of the political repercussions, the federal authorities never sent her to jail (Merrill 1986, 71).

Martha loved hearing about such daringness. She discovered that the area was a hotbed for other independent women. Antoinette Brown Blackwell of Henrietta, a nearby town, became America's first female ordained minister. On a visit to the area, Lucretia Mott joined Elizabeth Cady Stanton and other local women who organized the now famous Seneca Falls Women's Rights Convention in 1848 and issued the Declaration of Sentiments calling for women's right to vote. Of the one hundred people who signed that document, five were Rochester women, led by Amy Post, who had trekked fifty miles to be there.

Two weeks later, these Rochesterians took responsibility for organizing another meeting on August 2, 1848, in Rochester. This meeting, as historian Nancy Hewitt documented in *Women's Activism and Social Change,* was called to "consider the Rights of women; Politically, Socially,

Religiously and Industrially" (1984, 130–131). The emphasis clearly was on *rights* as distinct from *social evils* or *conditions* affecting women's rights, which was a key part of the Seneca Falls discussion. The Rochester session was a radical meeting; a woman presided. In her article "Feminist Friends" Hewitt revealed that Elizabeth Cady Stanton and Lucretia Mott almost left the meeting because of such boldness (1995, 34).

Martha and others found Rochester and its upstate sister communities to be centers for social change. In August 1848, Rochester women organized a Working Woman's Protective Union, declaring that women were entitled to be in the workplace just as men were. Sarah Burtis became a role model, taking a job as the community's first female store clerk, even though she was married and had seven children (Hewitt 1995, 35).

First in 1848, and again in 1860, the New York State legislature addressed women's right to own and control property. In 1866, the Equal Rights Association was formed in Rochester; it disappointingly argued that women would need to yield to the voting rights of the Negro man. Another group was then formed to fight for women's suffrage (Hewitt 1995, 36).

Education also became a Rochester battlefield for women. In 1883, Henry Morgan, an ethnologist who wrote *The League of the Iroquois*, died and left $80,000 to the University of Rochester to educate women. It was two more decades before women were admitted to the university—and only after Susan B. Anthony promoted the cause. In order to meet the dollar goal the university had established for women's admission, Anthony pledged her own insurance policy, and women were admitted.

All of this social unrest likely spoke to Martha's sense of right. She was discovering that spunk, belief in a cause, and the stomach for a long crusade to better women's lives were Rochester-made qualities. The city seemed to be full of pragmatic innovators and idealists with whom she could identify—as women, as visionaries, as businesspeople. Martha must have wondered where a community developed such a tolerance for social agitation.

From Rochester's early days, religious groups played an important role. The most established group was Rochester's Episcopal church.

Other religious groups migrated into the area. The revivalists came in 1820, followed by the Mormons in 1827. In the 1840s the Seventh Day Adventists came, as did the Spiritualists. In fact, in the late 1840s the Fox sisters, who lived in nearby Hydesville, began that movement after they heard rappings (communications from the dead).

A smaller group of determined Quakers with lofty ideals was to fundamentally influence the social consciousness of the Rochester community. By 1825, they numbered nearly six hundred; they grew by attracting friends and relatives. According to Katherine Anthony, one of Susan B. Anthony's biographers, the more radical group of Quakers, called the Hicksites, "were the backbone of the liberal thought and action in Rochester" (1975, 87). They were lower-middle-class folks, idealists and tenacious farmers, many of whom became shopkeepers and grass-roots reformers. They promoted temperance, abolition of slavery, land reform, and Indian and women's rights.

In *Women's Activism and Social Change,* Nancy Hewitt recorded that "Rochester hosted more antislavery, woman's rights, dress reform and spiritualists conventions and rallies than did neighboring cities, primarily as a result of the migratory patterns of some two dozen Hicksite families and the local citizens took note, be it in honorific or horrific tones" (1984, 36). They had an effect. While Abraham Lincoln won the presidency with a minority of the popular vote, Rochester gave him a majority of its vote.

In this community of independent thinkers, Martha listened to and digested rebellious thoughts, still performing menial tasks such as making beds and preparing food for the household. A year after her arrival, Martha's employers literally left her. On August 7, 1883, the Hoveys sold their residence to Luella J. Roberts, a native New Englander; Martha remained as if she, as a good servant, were part of the real estate.

Her new employers were attractive, affluent, and emotionally needy. Mrs. Roberts was described in Surrogate Court estate papers as "short and fleshy" by a nephew, Maurice Flanders, and "a born lady, dignified" by a cousin, Mrs. Mary Willoughby (Flanders 1933, 1702; Willoughby 1933, 1702). Another cousin, Blanche Wentworth, described Luella's husband, Owen, as stout, gray-haired, and dapper (1933, 1702).

Both Luella and Owen, who were childless, had been orphaned at a young age, and each bore the emotional scars and insecurities such a trauma causes. Fulfilling their household and emotional needs became Martha's responsibility. Mrs. Roberts and Martha particularly bonded because each had been abandoned by her mother. In Martha's case, her childhood servitude forced the separation, while Mrs. Roberts' mother deserted her when she was an infant.

According to Wentworth, Mrs. Roberts later stated that she "had no particular affection for any woman [her mother] who would go off and leave a baby" (1933, 1702); in fact Mrs. Roberts hungered for the unconditional love traditionally given by a mother. Having endured her mother's rejection, she then suffered another emotional blow; her beloved father died when she was quite young. Mrs. Roberts was then cared for by her father's half sister. In 1851 Luella married Owen Roberts, a family connection, who inherited wealth (Willoughby 1933, 1702; Gammon 1933, 1702).

Born on different sides of the tracks, Martha and Mrs. Roberts each survived an emotionally battering childhood, and each remained hungry for affection. Finding in each other a source of love previously denied, they developed an intense codependence. Martha, the servant, became the adoring, trustworthy daughter committed to Mrs. Roberts. Mrs. Roberts became Martha's surrogate mother, someone she could, and would, protect for the rest of her life.

Martha found a new family. Initially the trio formed an outwardly loving relationship in which the Robertses commanded and Martha responded; she was rewarded with praise, support, and a sense of belonging.

Since Mr. Roberts had investments in real estate and business, Martha likely was exposed to conversations about the local and national business climate. She learned that Rochester was a magnet to many. In 1882, Rochester was a bustling city full of wealth, business, independence, and the flexibility to adapt and prosper.

Rochester had a tradition of birthing new businesses that came to dominate its economy. Its access to the Genesee River's waterpower contributed to its early growth in flour milling. Then, as St. Louis started to dominate as the nation's leading wheat shipper, Rochester turned to flower and nursery stock production; later it became known for its shoes, men's clothing, optical and camera equipment, and many other specialties (Kelly 1934, 30).

The city offered great employment opportunities and experienced economic growth from these various industries. By the 1880s, the value of its production went from $10 million to $31 million, and the number of manufacturers more than doubled as Rochester tapped the skills of its entrepreneurial settlers. It was a community calling for business creation and encouraging Martha.

Yet, Martha was responsible for mundane household issues. Mrs. Roberts often was unwell. Advertisements in the February 2, 1882, issue of the *Democrat & Chronicle* promoted medicinal products including Mrs. Lydia Pinkham's Vegetable Compound (containing 18 percent alcohol for women to sip) and Dr. Benson's Skin Care (6). In 1879, Hulbert H. Warner was a prominent businessman, who was called Mr. Patent Medicine Man. Rochester was full of his claims for medical remedies. Martha heard of these "cures," but kept looking for something else. She was uncertain what it was.

At the same time, there was a spiritual component lacking in both Mrs. Roberts and Martha's lives. Martha was looking for something that would link her to God in a more direct and healthful way. She heard about Christian Science, a relatively new religion officially founded in 1879 by Mary Baker Eddy. That it was founded by a woman made it distinct to begin with; its premise and structure were fundamentally different from the traditional hierarchical religions Martha had known.

Christian Science churches operated as democracies, with no formal ministry. The congregation elected lay readers who read predetermined passages selected by Eddy; often those readers included women. The Mother Church handled central operations, but local churches had great freedom, allowing believers to pursue their own spiritual journeys. Individual experiences were shared with the congregation at healing meetings held on Wednesday evenings.

Stories spread about how Eddy built on her unhealthy past and articulated a different spiritual road for herself and others. Ultimately,

Eddy defined a new religion—Christian Science. She believed faith in the power of God could help heal maladies of the body. Mrs. Eddy trained others to guide would-be believers through their spiritual journeys and she called them "healing practitioners."

Intrigued, but consumed with other priorities, Martha focused on her job. Within the house, Mrs. Roberts was in charge. Martha attended to her duties, which included dressing Mrs. Roberts' hair. Soon Mrs. Roberts' friends began clamoring for Martha to clean and dress their hair, as well as massage their scalps and perform facials as only she could. All the while, the would-be entrepreneur was making her secret-formula tonic in her room. When the Robertses discovered what she was doing, they wholeheartedly supported her efforts and encouraged her to use their tool shed behind the house for manufacturing her tonic.

Where would all this lead Martha? How and where would she go into business? The Robertses' friends clearly wanted her to continue to care for their hair in the privacy of their homes. That was the way of the times. Either a servant cared for her mistress's hair or an independent hairdresser came to the home and dressed her hair. Such hairdressers often traveled to spas visited by their well-to-do customers, including Saratoga Springs and even Palm Beach.

That was not the life Martha wanted. She wanted stature equal to the entrepreneurial men of Rochester. She wanted a presence, a dignity, a different option. If she remained a servant, her footing would never be equal, nor would she have the resources to change her lifestyle. She needed something that did not exist.

When Susan B. Anthony preached that "a condition of dependency, pecuniary or political, can not [sic] bring about the best development of any individual or any class" (Anthony 1975, vii), Martha, then a noncitizen, did not identify with the power of the vote. Rather, she interpreted the empowerment message differently—business ownership could provide the path for her own and others' economic empowerment.

In evaluating her options, Martha determined that the emerging women's hair care business provided her with a unique opportunity as an entrepreneur with little money. Large operators had yet to stake their claim to the business. In fact, few public hair and skin care salons existed, and there were none in Rochester. Since Martha had a unique product and scientific knowledge, she hoped she had the keys to a successful enterprise.

First, though, she had to evaluate the market's receptivity to her tonic and generate some needed dollars. In 1887, Martha decided to pretest one of her products. According to *Golden Memories,* she asked a neighbor and friend, Mrs. Allen, to sell the Harper tonic by going from house to house (1938, 5, 7). People bought the tonic and liked it. What next?

Inspired by Rochester's other successful ventures, Martha tried to think big, and hired professional help to launch her operation. She turned to John Van Voorhis, a prominent local attorney. White-haired and courtly, he had been a local Congressman from 1879 to 1883 (and would serve again from 1893 to 1895). Van Voorhis had represented several successful entrepreneurs, including George Selden, who, though known as the father of the automobile, lost his right to his patents in a bitter court fight brought by Henry Ford. Van Voorhis also represented advocates for social justice including Susan B. Anthony, Frederick Douglass, and the Seneca Nation.

Whether Susan B. Anthony referred Martha to the Van Voorhis law firm or not, we do not know. Since the community knew the firm was where to go for social advocacy, Martha knew of Van Voorhis, sought him out, and came to trust him. Ultimately, his son Eugene became her attorney, and she retained the law firm for decades.

Before meeting with the Van Voorhis firm, Martha had to plan for the business. There were fundamental questions to be answered. What would her business look like—would it be a door-to-door operation? How would she attract a loyal customer base? How would she establish credibility with her targeted market of well-to-do people? How could she best introduce a public beauty salon when only prostitutes were identified with painted faces?

Slowly an image emerged. She would establish a salon where men and women would come to have their hair "dressed," their scalps relaxed, their skin massaged, their inner beauty brought out. And, of course, they would benefit from Martha's magical tonic. She would encourage them to wash their hair more frequently, perhaps by coming to her shop. She would need a chair, a bowl, a sink. She realized she needed to accumulate an inventory of her unique hair tonic as well as dollars to pay for the venture.

In 1888, trying to ready her business while keeping Mr. and Mrs. Roberts happy and the house clean and organized, Martha worked round the clock. To produce the tonic, she spent her evenings mixing her secret formula. The workload obviously overwhelmed her, but we have few details. *Golden Memories* simply indicates that she collapsed from exhaustion (1938, 7).

To launch her business, Martha had to get well quickly. Christian Science provided the key to her recovery, and thereafter remained a powerful influence on her life. When Martha was ill, she was introduced to Mrs. Helen Pine Smith, an approved Christian Science practitioner (*Golden Memories* 1938, 7). Records of the Mother Church in Boston indicate that Smith, a Rochesterian, had just completed her studies with Mrs. Eddy in March (Smith 1997). As a healing practitioner, Smith was available, day or night, to help people in pain reach out to God and go beyond their physical ailments to find spiritual healing.

Martha engaged Smith for such services, and just as a doctor would be, Smith was paid for her work. Smith and Martha likely prayed together to better understand God, the Divine Mind, and to yield to God's healing power. As they talked, Smith may have reminded Martha that each person was a reflection of God. Martha, therefore, was important.

Reportedly, three days after her first visit with Smith, Martha's strength returned. Regular visits to her Christian Science practitioner followed. They must have been greatly valued, because fifty years later, Martha recorded in *Golden Memories* that those visits cost her precious dollars she had saved for her business (1938, 7).

For Martha, those visits brought much more than a momentary recovery. She became enamored of Christian Science and its philosophy. She learned that Christian Scientists refer to God as Mother-Father because they believe God possesses both female and male qualities. Christian Science doctrine suggests that each person has a unique composition of nongender-limited qualities and a distinct way of expressing those qualities. The composite forms the Divine Mind. Over a century

Mrs. Helen Smith, the Christian Science
practitioner responsible for Martha's rapid
recovery in 1888 and her subsequent
commitment to Christian Science.
Courtesy of Golden Memories.

ago, such beliefs were revolutionary. Christian Scientists believed in the
equality of men and women.

While Mary Baker Eddy primarily focused on spiritual matters, she
also commented on gender discrimination in *Science and Health:* "Civil
law establishes very unfair differences between the rights of the two
sexes. Christian Science furnishes no precedent for such injustice, and
civilization mitigates it in some measure" (1934, 63).

Such support for women had to be affirming to Martha; Christian
Science made her feel that she was relevant, and shared her philosophy

that women did not need men to define them or make them whole. Instead, Martha was encouraged to believe that she was significant because *she* was God's expression. By finding Christian Science and experiencing the camaraderie of people who supported her and her right to be valued, Martha's soul was calmed and her ambition was propelled toward a distinct model influenced by Christian Science values.

Christian Scientists were told to act kindly, in order to emulate the model of God in their behavior. According to Christian Science, exercises of power and abuse were not part of God's model; sharing, love, kindness, and support were.

Among such believers, Martha no longer had to hide her values. Her harsh childhood, her abandonment, her lower-class existence surely left emotional scars and unmet needs, along with imposed feelings of inadequacy. Her abusive childhood was real, but insignificant in God's eye. The material world that bound her to a doomed destiny was a false god and one she could reject; there was a spiritual sphere of love and support awaiting her, and Martha was eager for both.

Christian Science provided Martha with companions of like mind, a network of people who cared about her, and a philosophical and spiritual framework on which to build the next phase of her life, in particular her business. As she learned about the bold and daring journey of Christian Science's founder, Mary Baker Eddy, Martha likely identified with how Eddy, a sickly woman, had overcome her poor health and changed the course of her life. The possibility that there was a divine force able to free people of their emotional and physical burdens fascinated Martha. The message was clear. Others, including women, had suffered, but that suffering was momentary. Christian Science became a positive force in her life and that of other Rochesterians.

According to local church records, Practitioner Smith's sister, Sarah Pine, was the early teacher of the First Church of Christ, Scientist, in Rochester. Interest in Christian Science grew, and members met in each other's parlors until a church was organized. While people like Martha might initially have been attracted to the bodily healing aspect of Christian Science, spiritual wholeness was the ultimate goal. Christian Science authority Robert Peel reminded followers that the focus was on the spiritual, not the material, since "matter . . . was a false mode of consciousness" (1988, 20). The power of the spiritual, of God's force that forms the Divine Mind, was what Mary Baker Eddy wanted her practitioners to accept. She stated in *Science and Health*, "The Mind governs the body, not partially but wholly" (1934, 111).

For a determined woman like Martha, who was trying to overcome emotional trials and financial oppression, Christian Science made sense. Such a belief system explained her concept that external looks were not what determined beauty. To Martha, being healthy was fundamental to being beautiful. She had accepted Christian Science's belief that spirit controlled health, then taken it another step to support her emerging business concept. For Martha, the new believer, it was not a major jump to believe that healthy natural products were consistent with her newfound religious beliefs.

Devout Christian Scientists might wince at Martha's interpretations. Eddy's definition of spirit did not require that it be an inner spirit; in fact, she envisioned an essence that was not limited or contained within. Eddy conceived that there was a loving spirit which created a pattern of behavior. That spirit transcended all material sense. The body was momentary.

While Martha might not have been a Christian Science scholar, she found great joy among Christian Scientists; they appreciated and valued women leaders. No matter that her religious association again made her an outsider to many; she was used to being different.

In Rochester, Martha Matilda Harper had found a new home and family, a supportive community of like-minded believers in entrepreneurship, women's rights, and spiritual emancipation. She was ready to take the next step.

CHAPTER  FOUR

Launching Her Business

THE YEAR 1888 WAS A MOMENTOUS ONE for Rochester and for Martha. The first Episcopalian deaconess was ordained in Rochester by the bishop. Rochester's park system was established. A new bank, which ultimately became Central Trust Company, opened. Then two Rochester residents launched their new businesses, both of which would become international in scope. Only one, however, would live on in history.

George Eastman, age thirty-three, introduced his camera—and the KODAK name—with $1 million of venture capital (*The Biographical Record of the City of Rochester and Monroe County, New York* 1902, 437). George Eastman's story and legacy are legendary. Martha Matilda Harper's are not.

When Martha, two years Eastman's junior, turned the doorknob of the elegant Powers Building's Room 516, she had invested $360—her life savings. As Martha crossed the threshold to open her Harper Hairdressing Parlor on August 21, she was changing the course of the hair care industry (*Harper Method Progress* Aug. 1930, 12–13).

Nothing happened easily for Martha. Simply to rent space in the Powers Building had been a struggle. One can only imagine the pompous Powers reacting to this female Canadian immigrant, short in stature and insignificant in social class, who proposed to rent a room for her audacious new beauty scheme because the Powers Building must house Rochester's first hairdressing shop and manufacturing center for its products.

Likely Martha argued that her valuable formula and training in healthful hair care would give Rochester the opportunity to break with the tradition

39

Daniel Powers, owner of the Powers Building, eventually
agreed to house her shop, the city's first public beauty parlor.
Courtesy of the First National Bank.

of having rich women's hair privately dressed. It was time for Rochester
to be a leader and introduce the concept of public beauty care.

To Powers, a *nouveau riche* entrepreneur who tenaciously held to
societal custom, it was too daring a scheme for him to risk his reputation
and expose his building's clientele to such brashness. Like many Victo-
rians, he believed that powder, rouge, and other cosmetics were inap-
propriate for proper women. As noted beauty consultant Florence E.
Wall put it, they were "classed with cigarettes, narcotics, and alcoholic
drinks as the perfect lady's sure skids to perdition" (1948, 2). Powers
likely thought that Martha's idea would break the social etiquette and
lead to an unacceptable use of beauty products. To him, her public

beauty salon idea appeared to be a dangerous step toward exposing what properly belonged hidden in the home.

Martha's concept was unilaterally rejected. Powers was convinced that her beauty shop surely would attract trollops and prostitutes. Her reassurance that she would never let such women into her shop could not overcome Powers's fundamental concern. She wanted him to believe that she would not promote the clownlike use of makeup. He did not. She persisted, claiming that her methods would change the world and improve hair and skin health. Powers dismissed her.

Determined, Martha astutely turned to John Van Voorhis, an important tenant in the Powers Building. Significantly, she realized that to achieve her goal of becoming a legitimate tenant in the Powers Building, she needed Van Voorhis's help; perhaps more significantly, she was willing to pay for that help. As a servant girl, Martha had observed the power of influence, money, proper connections, and the art of networking. She had watched carefully, and she used the techniques she had learned to achieve her goal.

Van Voorhis's assignment was to get Martha and her business into the building. A well-known supporter of the underdog, he was likely mesmerized by Martha's self-confidence, her vision to change women's lives as workers, her passion for transforming her own life, and her wonderful head of hair.

John Van Voorhis understood Powers's sensitivity and business self-interest. He made a compelling case on Martha's behalf, and Powers yielded; Martha could rent space! There was a condition. Powers would allow her to occupy Room 516 of his building only on a month-to-month basis, in case he had to evict her if her business attracted the wrong kind of women (Beeney 1973, 3C). Regardless of this vulnerability, Martha believed she had won. She was about to open her business in the most desirable location in Rochester.

More determined than ever, Martha realized her business had to work; every decision was critical, especially in light of the social mores of the time. The mainstream perception was that most women did not belong in business, where they might learn self-reliance, engage in the impure world of money, and be encouraged to develop their mercenary instincts; better they should devote themselves to family and religious concerns. A leading professor of psychological medicine at the time, Dr. R. Frederick Marvin, defined unhealthy female behavior thus: "For a woman to believe that she can exercise her will in order to accomplish a 'mission in the world' is a symptom of disease" (Braude 1989, 159). During this era, American men theoretically had unlimited opportunity to succeed by working hard.

Martha's plans would make her an anomaly. According to the Victorian code and institutions, women were discouraged from such dreams. Alice Kessler-Harris's book *Women Have Always Worked* established how societal forces isolated women from productive work, the sphere of influence. Sociologist Alice Rossi observed that Victorian white women, by not being a part of the workforce and with less household responsibility (given industrialization), were "effectively cut off from participation in the significant work of their society" (quoted in Kessler-Harris 1981, 13).

Publications often suggested that when women did go into business, such pursuit was the result of necessity. Women might become business owners following the death of a mate, father, or brother. That is what Frances Willard's nineteenth-century career guidebook, *Occupations for Women,* implied about women's entry into entrepreneurial positions. Among the women cited in the book was Helen A. Whittier, president of two of the largest cotton factories in the country. Whittier *happened* into the business because her father, the original factory owner, passed the business on to her when her brother, his intended successor, unexpectedly died.

Death of a brother also *allowed* Amanda M. Lougee to come out of the closet; she no longer had to be the silent partner in the family's rubber "gossamer" factory. Under her leadership, the business expanded dramatically. It employed 275 people, and had offices in Chicago, Boston, and New York City. Death of a husband *permitted* Nellie Russell Kimball of nearby Dunkirk, New York, to run her husband's coal and wood yard (Willard 1897, 355–358). Willard's examples of successful female business owners underscore the reluctance of society to have women intentionally run large businesses. Rather, women might be *granted* such an opportunity because of the death of a family member.

Clearly, Martha's situation did not resemble those female manufacturers; she inherited nothing and was a poor, single immigrant woman with dreams of building her own enterprise.

The business experiences of custom milliners and dressmakers provided Martha with a different and, perhaps, more relevant model. These women, unlike shopkeepers and boardinghouse owners, worked their way up through mastery of their craft. Wendy Gamber, an authority on female clothing entrepreneurs, suggested they were the "aristocrats among the clothing makers" (1997, 1). They capitalized on the division of a sex-segregated economy, learned a creative, skilled trade, earned good money from it, and had the possibility of being a proprietor. The majority of those proprietors were upwardly mobile, white, working-class women, largely native-born (1997, 2–5, 26, 34).

These proprietors were the same age as Martha, in their thirties or forties, when they started their businesses. Like her, the majority remained single by choice, understanding the risk marriage represented to their economic and personal independence (Gamber 1997, 32). They seized a trade that allowed them business access to their female customers. It would have been unseemly for men to fit Victorian women for their clothes.

Martha understood that her products and trade, promoting healthy hair and skin care, demanded new skills not widely known in American shops. On the other hand, beauty and hair care was a field in which women had the potential to excel, for precisely the same societal restrictions that gave them the advantage in the clothing industries. For men to publicly dress women's hair or touch women's skin would have been socially unacceptable, particularly in Rochester, New York. Still, the obstacles were enormous.

Most of the dressmaking and millinery shops had limited capital, and they were often short-lived. Their limited production was being undercut by the prefabrication and wholesaling of women's clothing, an industry dominated by men. These women's shops ultimately gave way to sweatshops employing thousands of dressmakers.

The success of Madame Ellen (Nell) Curtis Demorest, a nineteenth-century businesswoman, provided multiple lessons for Martha, including the possibility of a female being an innovator and the impact of marriage. Nell and her sister Kate operated a millinery shop, initially funded by her father, in Troy, New York. By the 1850s, they had moved their successful operation to New York City, where Nell met her future husband, a master marketer, crusader, and inventor named William Jennings Demorest. Upon marrying in 1858, Nell formed a powerful business partnership with her husband, which made history and enriched them both. Nell was an innovator of women's corsets and crinolines during the mid-1800s. Later she revolutionized the garment industry by creating paper patterns at a time when sewing machines were becoming more popular.

According to Ishbell Ross's biography of Demorest, *Crusades and Crinolines,* this idea came from watching her black servant "cut out a dress from crude brown wrapping-paper patterns" (1963, 21). Nell's inventiveness allowed American women to have high fashion at lower costs (Ross 1963, 24).

William Demorest came from Brighton, a community adjacent to Rochester. Upon his marriage to Nell, he took over business operations and promotions, while Nell took care of their children and maintained the fashionableness of their salon and pattern design. She understood her role; Nell became the showpiece, the fashion oracle, while her husband ran the business, became the outspoken temperance crusader, and invented a variety of items, including sewing machines. Nell often worked behind the scenes to promote women's rights.

One of the offshoots of Nell's business was *Demorest's Illustrated Monthly,* edited by Jane Croly. The magazine promoted fashion, and even offered sample patterns to readers; it also encouraged women's independence, pursuit of education, and work opportunities. Surely Martha would have heard about, read, and/or been inspired by that popular publication before its demise in 1887.

As Ross details, in 1868 Croly, with the help of others, including Nell, organized the Sorosis Club because women reporters were prohibited from joining the male-only New York Press Club. The Sorosis Club's purpose was to advance women "'through unity and co-operation'" (Ross 1963, 93). This was the start of the women's club movement, which did not spread to Rochester until the 1890s.

Thus Martha was at least vaguely aware of other women's entrepreneurial activities. Although she might have known from her Germanic doctor friend that public hairdressing parlors operated in Europe, it is unclear how much she knew about early hairdressing operations in other American cities. Kathy Peiss, in her documentary on the beauty industry, *Hope in a Jar*, showed that in 1872, Mary Williams, a daughter of former slaves, operated a hairdressing parlor in Columbus, Ohio, that catered to both black and white customers (1998, 63). In 1879 Madam Thompson had a successful salon in New York City. There were likely other women-owned shops, but few historical records survive. In 1888 the male-dominated Hair Dealer's Association was formed; it included mostly equipment and product manufacturers, and wigmakers, more store owners than salon proprietors. Martha did not join this group; instead she went out on her own to play a pioneering role in this new industry.

Such independence is often characteristic of entrepreneurs. It was not until December 19, 1887, that the independent men of the Rochester community established the Rochester Chamber of Commerce. As various local industries, including manufacturers of carriages, lamps, furniture, tobacco products, women's shoes, men's clothing, musical instruments, and nurseries, boomed, issues uniting them, such as appropriate bankruptcy laws, became more important. One hundred and fifty men paid the $20 annual dues. A battle for President ensued, and ultimately Hubert H. Warner was elected.

Warner's rise from medical showman to corporate leader had been spectacular. In 1884 his Rochester operation was the largest medical lab in the world, according to local sources. It was housed in his eight-story building on St. Paul Boulevard. He was a model, but not one Martha wanted to follow. When he became the first President of the Rochester Chamber of Commerce, a notable metamorphosis occurred, turning him from a flamboyant supersalesman into Mr. Establishment. A wizard at merchandising, Warner built the Warner Observatory for the astronomer Lewis Swift and cleverly had a label from the Warner Safe Liver Pills box serve as an admission ticket, thereby suggesting a scientific credibility for his product (McKelvey 1980, 92). By 1898, Warner, in spite of his cleverness, was broke.

Martha had a different style and a far different long-term goal. Because she wanted to succeed, and that was hard enough for a woman, she had no inclination for flamboyancy. Yet, Martha had learned from her Uncle John about the value of belonging to groups. Although the date is not known, according to the Rochester Chamber of Commerce magazine, *Rochester Commerce,* Martha was the first woman to join the business group (1954, 21).

Martha's initiative did not stop with her Chamber membership. When envisioning her business, she decided her operation needed a visual image, something the world could identify with. The source of such inspiration is a mystery. Was it her quarter of a century of dreaming of a different future, or was it the encouraging words of Elizabeth Cady Stanton and Susan B. Anthony that set the broader context of what her business represented?

In 1881, while Anthony and Stanton were encouraging women to think about political enfranchisement, they understood the overall importance of independence. They admonished their audiences, "We would warn the young women of the coming generation against man's advice as to their best interests. . . . Women must lead the way to [their] own enfranchisement" (Freedman 1995, 75).

However it happened, Martha envisioned a business deserving of significant symbolism and legal protection. As if she foresaw the future she would create, she chose for its logo a horn of plenty. According to the *Harper Method Textbook,* the horn of plenty projected the "bounteous financial rewards that would accrue to a servant girl who was wise enough to become [a] Harperite" (1926, 1). The horn of plenty was a shrewd choice. It was a nonthreatening image with a very serious nonverbal message—feed yourself; free yourself.

Wisely, Martha decided to have the logo trademarked and registered to her business. On June 5, 1888, Eugene Van Voorhis, John's son, took on his first legal assignment and accomplished the task. The firm had also patented her Mascaro Tonique for the Hair on March 22, 1888. With the right place to operate her business, her patent for her product, and her clever logo protected, Martha next needed to make a fundamental marketing decision. How would she attract customers to the community's first public hairdressing and skin treatment salon?

Bertha Farquhar, former servant girl,
became Martha's first assistant.
Courtesy of Betty Wheeler.

Martha, the household servant, understood the importance of impressions and the inclinations of affluent women. To encourage women
to try her new service, she wanted them to have a luxurious experience.
The shop had to look appealing and to reassure her patrons that it met
their sanitary standards. Bertha Farquhar, Martha's first assistant, recalled in the *Harper Method Progress,* "The reception room had a blue
chenille carpet on the floor and Miss Harper insisted that [we] thor-
oughly clean underneath the edges and in the corners. [According to
Farquhar, Martha would say] 'Now, Bertha, you know we have a lot of
fussy customers, and if they see dirt they will think we don't do our

work right'" (Aug. 1930, 14). Clearly Martha understood the power of impressions and the critical need to have a consistent image; she knew that if the Harper Method was to be identified with quality service, it needed a quality environment.

While managing a salon, Martha was also pioneering a new industry of hair and skin care for women based on scientific principles including cleanliness, stimulation, and exercise. In *The Scientific Care of the Hair and Scalp*, she wrote:

> The whole Harper Method [was] . . . developed from . . . the . . . principle of "health first." With the scalp properly cleaned, a vigorous flow of blood coursing through its tissues and free from disease, the way [was] cleared for a healthful, luxuriant growth of hair which is the first requirement in any woman's claim to beauty. . . . Beauty and health are inseparable. . . . The laws of cleanliness, nourishment, exercise and breathing must be observed. (1932, 1,4)

Martha also asserted that beauty was linked to both good health and spiritual wholeness. Her philosophy was captured in the *Harper Method Textbook* when she stated that beauty went "deeper even than health and cleanliness." She believed that "human beauty is a result of proper condition of mind as well as surface and form" (*Harper Method Textbook* 1926, 216). Her beliefs, clearly influenced by Christian Science, defied society's long held traditions of beauty, the proper role of women in business, and how women might control their own attractiveness.

To succeed, Martha, who needed customers, capitalized on a ready resource—her hair. When a photographer asked to take her picture, she negotiated a clever agreement. Martha allowed her photo to be taken, and in exchange she received a copy. There she stood—dressed as a Victorian gentlewoman with cascading floor-length hair. That photo of Martha became her shop's first advertisement.

She pasted that compelling image, designed to draw attention, on the glass panel of the shop's outer door. It served as an invitation to stop in (*Golden Memories* 1938, 9). She hoped most people would be intrigued

This photo of Martha served as her shop's first
advertisement and was used for years after to promote
the effectiveness of the Harper Method.
Courtesy of Golden Memories.

and would ask, Who is that woman? She wanted people walking down the marbled corridors of the Powers Building's fifth floor to inquire about her services, and they did.

Golden Memories also recorded that "Her first patron was an artist from an office nearby" (1938, 9). High-class women urged Martha to come to their homes and not break with tradition. She refused. She had to sell this new approach in order to succeed. She also knew that Daniel Powers was waiting for her shop to attract the wrong kind of woman, and she took drastic measures to assure her targeted market was not jeopardized. Her assistant Bertha Farquhar recalled in the Harper newsletter, "Her method of eliminating undesired patrons [was] rather amusing. Women of dubious reputation were somewhat embarrassed to find payment for service refused and still further chagrined to be politely, but firmly requested not to come back again by [Martha]" (*Harper Method Progress* Aug. 1930, 13).

Days passed, and Martha waited for the right kind of customers; they came slowly and infrequently. From *Golden Memories* we learn what ultimately happened. "It was a music teacher who finally turned the tide. He moved in next door without space for a waiting room. Canny Martha Matilda offered hers and soon the mothers of his pupils were having her do their hair while the music lessons went on" (1938, 9–10).

Daniel Powers noticed that the local society women were making the Harper Shop the talk of the town. Since he was first and foremost a shrewd businessman, he wanted her to sign a long-term lease.

Without a moment's pause, Martha rejected his offer and assured him that operating on a month-to-month basis would be just fine. Though she was hungry for success, her principles (or was it her pride?) would not let her accept what she had so eagerly pursued. According to Beeney, Martha Matilda Harper was the only tenant who refused to sign a lease, and she remained in the Powers Building for fifty years (1973, 3C)!

Meanwhile, Martha made other significant decisions about her future. She chose to be an entrepreneur at the shop by day and to return to the Roberts household at night to help Mrs. Roberts. As Martha explained, "Mr. Roberts was a drinking man and . . . [Mrs. Roberts] was afraid of him. She could not get a girl and I stayed to protect her" (M. Harper 1933, 1702).

Martha again assumed the role of protector, just as she had done for her real mother. Loyalty, love, and support, the qualities she so desperately hungered for, she gave to Mrs. Roberts. It was a symbiotic relationship, with each feeding the other's insecurity and anxiety. Wherever her future took her, Martha assured Mrs. Roberts she would not desert her, and Mrs. Roberts held her emotionally bound to that pledge.

Ironically, as Martha was declaring her economic independence, she was pulled into an emotional whirlpool that held the Robertses and her captive. Other wives, sisters, and daughters of the era shared the vulnerability of their husbands', fathers', or brothers' drinking problems. Some of those women joined the temperance movement. Martha and Mrs. Roberts joined no such movement; instead, Mrs. Roberts turned to Martha, and together they endured the pain, intimidation, and tantrums resulting from Mr. Roberts's alcoholic bouts.

Yet even this depressing relationship did not deter Martha from pursuing her dream of reinventing her future. She noticed that women were being educated. By 1882 at least twenty-five colleges and universities admitted women. Martha, previously without means and education, decided to invest her shop's first profits in herself.

The *Harper Method Textbook* states that she hired tutors to give her a broad liberal arts education, including sociology, history, and the arts. Once she mastered these courses, Martha attended evening classes at the University of Rochester, which were open to women (*Harper Method Textbook* 1926, 213). Fortunately, the college, located on University Avenue, was just blocks from the Roberts home. Its convenient access helped Martha pursue formal classes and thereby improve her future in spite of past schooling deficiencies or societal assumptions of women's place.

Her business grew. Prominent women, her targeted clientele, became her customers, and Martha's reputation spread not only among the elite but also among the suffragists. Susan B. Anthony was responsible for that, although no records have been found that explain how or when they met. According to Edward Harrison, editor of the *Rochester Commerce*, Susan B. Anthony became Martha's steady supporter and customer, and cited her business as a prime example of a woman determining her own destiny (1963, 19).

Anthony, with her simple bun of silver hair, enjoyed Harper's revital-
izing hair treatments. The focus was on the healthful treatments, not on
styling. As Harper executive Earl Freese recalled during a 1956 dedication ceremony at the University of Rochester's Susan B. Anthony dormitory, "Many times after the beauty work was finished and the shop
was closed, they tarried on together into the late hours talking eagerly
about the plight of womanhood in their times. [Anthony was] struggling to bring . . . [the vote] to women and Martha [was] striving to
help women establish themselves in the business world" (1956, 1).

Anthony introduced other national and local suffragists to the Harper
Method, including Mrs. Josephine Sargent Force from Rochester. Force,
first tried the Method because, in her own words, "I was brought up
a suffragist and was interested in Miss Harper and her work and was
interested in anything women were doing" (1933, 1702).

Eventually, business became so brisk that Martha hired assistants.
Farquhar recalled what the shop was like in those early days: "Miss
Harper was known as the best bang cutter in western New York. Our
row of three chairs was always full. I brought the customer in, put on
her bib, wet the bang to straighten it and got her ready for Miss Harper's
scissors. How sharp they were and how they flew. It was work, work,
work, from early morning till late at night" (*Golden Memories* 1938, 9).

When demand forced Martha to hire others, she chose former servants. She felt connected with these women who had been domestics
like herself. They understood each other, and Martha perceptively realized how their training could foster her business. These were women
willing to take directions and used to giving loyal service, qualities she
required in order to grow and to distinguish her operation. She needed
these women; they became her daughters through shared life experiences. Together, they would change their worlds.

As a servant, Martha Matilda Harper had been taught to please. As
a businesswoman, Martha was a champion of the importance of customer satisfaction. As a pioneer in a new industry, she understood customers were essential partners in building her business. By recruiting
from the servant class, Martha ensured that her staff understood service

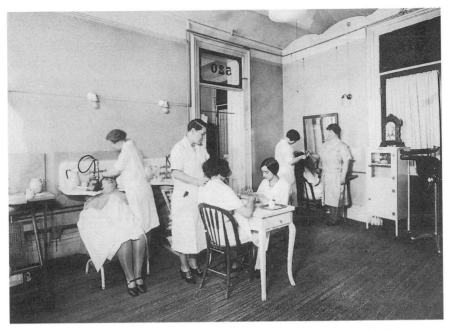

The Harper Shop. Demand for the Harper Method caused shop expansion in the Powers Building; the shop, originally in Room 516, came to include more rooms and many assistants. *Courtesy of Betty Wheeler.*

as a way of life. Her goal was to make "every patron a pleased advertisement" (*Golden Memories* 1938, 11).

Seventy years later, another Rochester business pioneer, Joseph C. Wilson, Chief Executive Officer of Xerox, stated the importance of the customer to Xerox; his words were considered bold and innovative for the 1960s. Some suggest that his visionary leadership helped Xerox become one of the first corporations to win the Baldridge Award for quality service. In a Xerox Historical Museum exhibit at Midtown Plaza in Rochester, Wilson's words were showcased: "In the long run, our customers are going to determine whether we have a job or whether we do not. Their attitude towards us is going to be the factor determining our success. Every Xerox person must resolve that their most important duty is to our customers."

Martha Matilda Harper would have smiled to hear her philosophy being taught seventy years after she first articulated the importance of the customer. In Lucille Huntington's profile of the Harper founder in the *Christian Science Monitor,* Martha's commitment to service was simply stated: "Build everything on service. If you give full measure of service, you will never want and your horn of plenty will overflow" (1946, 4).

Delighting all customers was Martha's goal. To do that, she understood the essentials: providing first-class service and skill, along with a well-trained and motivated staff in delightful surroundings. As captured in the *Harper Method Progress,* Martha understood that "prestige doesn't mean merely giving the best—it means making people proud to be known as patrons of your shop" (Sept.-Oct. 1927, 113).

Martha taught her operators that their job was to relax the patrons, uplift their spirits, calm their nerves, and restore their well-being. From the Harper textbook came these specific guidelines: "The Harper Operator['s] . . . thoughts [must be] centered on the one desire to serve her patron in the best possible way" (*Harper Method Textbook* 1926, 17). "So we calm our patron . . . from the very moment that [we greet her]—she begins to enjoy a comfort and an ease that casts aside all distracting influences" (*Harper Method Textbook* 1926, 12).

Martha understood that customer comfort was fundamental. Before Abraham Maslow, the social scientist who developed a hierarchy of needs, Martha Matilda Harper astutely understood that customers needed physical security and comfort. A *Fortune* article entitled "Potpourri" reported that Martha Matilda Harper designed the first reclining shampoo chair in the United States. It noted that "she began her work . . . with a procedure that was revolutionary. Instead of forcing her clients to bend forward over a wash basin, their faces trickling, their eyes soapy, she tipped them backward and kept them comfortable while she washed their hair" (1930, 94). Those early chairs were wicker and could recline at various angles. To accompany them, Harperite Betty Wheeler explained, Martha designed a unique marble sink that was cut out to fit the customer's neck perfectly.

Martha succeeded in delighting her customers, and demand for her services also grew through an informal but powerful network of customers. One such customer was Rochester society leader Mrs. Carolyn

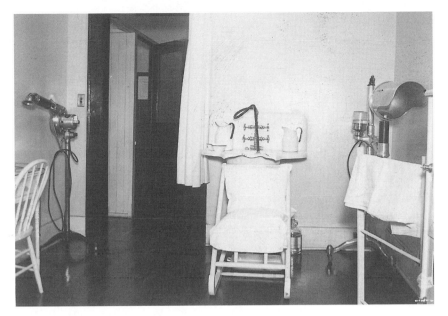

Harper chair. Martha's proprietary reclining, padded chair and contoured sink made the shampooing and skin treatment more comfortable for the customer. *Courtesy of Betty Wheeler.*

Lyon, who became enamored of the Method and advocated its use among her friends and contacts. One of those influential people, from Washington, D.C., was Mabel Graham Bell.

According to family recollection, the Bells visited Rochester's renowned Western New York Institute for the Deaf-Mute because Mr. Lyon, Carolyn's husband, had created the *Phonetic Manual*, a system for teaching the deaf to speak. Dr. Bell's father had earlier invented a visible speech system. The two families became good friends, and during the Bells' 1891 visit to Rochester, Mrs. Lyon took Mrs. Bell to the Harper Shop (D'Amanda 1997; Pancoast 1998). Other visitors came from Buffalo, Detroit, Chicago, and other major cities to experience the unique Harper Method. As Martha summed it up in *Golden Memories,* "Out-of-town friends were brought to [my] shop—for it was by now *the* place to go—and they in turn spread [my] fame at home"(1938, 10).

Such success led to a new crossroads: How to expand the business?

CHAPTER  FIVE

Franchising Her Concept

WOMEN FORCED MARTHA to make the critical business decision to expand her business, and women ultimately shaped the innovative model she developed. When her out-of-town patrons enthusiastically urged Martha to open shops in their hometowns, she astutely engaged them in market research and salesmanship. She asked them to bring back petitions from local women, committing them to patronize her shop if and when it opened. The signatures came in. From Chicago came signatures of the city's Who's Who, including "the reigning queen of Chicago society, Mrs. Potter Palmer" (Clune 1963, 2D).

This affirmation of support was certainly an important component of Martha's decision-making, but she needed to resolve more fundamental questions about how and why to expand. What was she really trying to do with her business? As she looked around, she saw other women running businesses; however, most of those enterprises were boarding-houses, single shops, or inherited operations. In 1890, women (including girls age ten or older) represented only 17 percent of all workers in America. Yet, the numbers were on the rise as the demographics changed—the flow of immigrant women, the smaller families, and the rising age at which women married (Brownlee and Elliot 1976, 23–25). In Rochester, thousands of women worked in shoe, clothing, and to-bacco factories instead of being servants.

Women's economic plight remained a serious issue. According to Mabel Collins Donnelly's study of the American Victorian woman, "The women factory worker worked for fifty-five or sixty hours a week, as her

Martha Harper the businesswoman.
As Martha became more successful, her hair was pinned up.
Courtesy of Golden Memories.

male co-workers did, but she worked for lower wages than a man received for the same job. If she was a servant, and seventy percent of
women workers in 1870 were domestics, she received a dollar or two
a week and room and board" (1986, 8).

Martha particularly identified with the lower-class women who worked
as servants. Being a maid was still an unattractive prospect, chosen
generally by immigrant girls or naïve country girls. Just as Martha had
experienced, the life of a servant was one of long hours and poor pay.
Elizabeth Roberts's study, *Women's Work,* established that in 1873, a
maid's day usually began at 8 A.M. and ran until 10 P.M. (1995, 20).

While Martha worked long hours, too, she was working for herself, and she understood what a difference that made. Perhaps her friend Susan B. Anthony reinforced her growing sense of self-empowerment, or perhaps Anthony merely affirmed Elizabeth Cady Stanton's sentiment: "Nothing strengthens the judgment and quickens the conscience like individual responsibility. Nothing adds such dignity to character as the recognition of one's self-sovereignty" (DuBois 1995, 46). Martha knew there was power in owning one's own business. Her dilemma was how to expand her business while simultaneously giving her sisters ownership opportunity.

The accepted approach to growing a business was to add more shops and more employees, all under singular control, which would naturally maximize one's individual or corporate profits. During this era, men thought their business success reflected Divine Will, although their day-to-day practices often ignored religious principles. In the 1890s, there were 4,047 millionaires, some of the most famous being the business tycoons Jay Gould, Cornelius Vanderbilt, John D. Rockefeller, Andrew Carnegie and J. P. Morgan. Vanderbilt dominated shipping, then railroads; Carnegie chose steel; and Rockefeller, oil. Without laws guarding against monopolies and conflicts of interest, and guaranteeing the rights of workers, opportunity was theirs for the taking. These potentates wheeled and dealed, succeeding through manipulative tactics that affected people's lives and fortunes.

The questionable business ethics of the era were described in Stewart H. Holbrook's *The Age of the Moguls*. Holbrook suggested that "the men of these times, even the best of them, made 'deals,' purchased immunity, and did other things which in 1860, or 1880, or even 1900, were considered no more than 'smart' . . . , but which under present-day rules, almost every man [who was a robber baron] would face a good hundred years in prison" (1953, ix). Winning and making money were the goals of these business magnates, who became absorbed in expanding their fortunes rather than in evaluating the means to fulfill their ambitions.

The more Martha learned about these men, the less she related to their styles, their principles, or their self-absorption. In manufacturing, Carnegie's approach was to cut prices, scoop the market, and watch costs. This required control. In contrast to Martha, loyalty was not high on

Carnegie's priority list. As Oliver Jensen noted, Carnegie had a pattern of using people; "[he] forced out some fifteen partners" (1967, 10).

John D. Rockefeller also believed in monopoly. He built his oil empire by buying out his competitors or leaving them in the dust. Linda Cornell's study of Ida Tarbell described Rockefeller's "nefarious" practices: "the negotiation of secret rebates with the railroads, the establishment of different sets of prices for different parts of the country, his ruthlessness in cutting out competition, the elaborate system of espionage (through bribing employees of both the railroads and competing plants) which kept him informed of competitors" (1966, 79).

As an increasingly devout Christian Scientist, Martha needed a business style different from what these men had perfected. Christian Science provided the model from which she built her alternative enterprise. Martha realized that when Mary Baker Eddy created her fundamentally different system of worship, she also created an overall operational guide, which she called the *Manual,* the constitution of her religion. Christian Science's headquarters and Mother Church, from which the administration and policy were controlled, were located in Boston; semiautonomous local churches formed a loosely knit federation. Possessing local autonomy, they had freedom of operation as long as they followed the Mother Church's procedural and spiritual directives.

Martha's exposure to Christian Science may have provided a mental framework for her new business structure, known today as franchising. Martha envisioned an ethics-based business model allowing for centralized control emanating from her. What was new was the idea that simultaneously there could be a network of satellite operations growing, serving her purposes, with all participants benefiting.

Exposure to other forces may also have influenced Martha's attempt to design a business to help other women. The political mobilization for women's rights and the growing popularity of women's clubs in Rochester may have inspired Martha. Several groups, such as the Wednesday Club, the Tuesday Reading Club, and the American History Class, had organized in 1890 with the goal of providing their members with self-improvement opportunities by strengthening their intellectual enrichment. Both they and the suffragists reinforced the joy of women acting collectively. The latter group was externally driven, and the former group built tight-knit associations of female self-interest.

Somehow Martha concluded that she could create an innovative way to mobilize her working-class sisters for their self-improvement, in a creative, principled entrepreneurial fashion. Her concept was simple: duplicate her shop, her method, her products, and her training throughout the country, even the world. Wherever customers went, they would find a Harper Hairdressing Salon and know what to expect.

Her system assured a consistency of service because each operator and franchisee learned and performed the Method; her way was the only way. For those who followed her path, Martha offered shop ownership. She set them up in business and insisted that they buy only her Harper-made products. Martha was paid to outfit Harper shops with Harper equipment and products. That reduced her need for expansion capital, which was often difficult for women business owners to raise.

It was a win-win arrangement; former servant women, "her girls," became entrepreneurs, and Martha remained their caring teacher. She changed their lives in a concrete way. It seemed a perfect solution for mutual growth, consistent with her moral code while capitalizing on her know-how, her proprietary products and methods, and her goal to replicate her shops around the world. Martha had test-marketed her business in Rochester, and an affluent clientele stood ready to patronize new shops in other communities.

Thomas S. Dicke's monumental work on franchising documented how in the mid-1800s, Singer Sewing Machine and McCormick Harvesting Machine Company used a franchise distribution system to penetrate their vertical product markets. McCormick hired agents who were given exclusive territories to sell his reapers; those agents also sold products not made by McCormick. Singer combined some company-owned branches with territorial agents to sell his sewing machines. These agents, too, could sell noncompeting goods. Ultimately, McCormick and Singer tried to change the agents from independent dealers to semi-independent ones (Dicke 1992, 7, 46, 47).

Martha's concept was fundamentally different from their system of selling products. Her system created a retail (or business format) franchise model that literally provided a blueprint for duplicating her retail hair and skin-care business; this meant women could successfully own and operate small businesses by following the Harper system. Martha explicitly taught her women how to go into her business. By deciding everything fundamental—shop location, product lines and services, and targeted market—Martha offered a formula for business success. She personally trained women to be effective Harper operators and owners. Nothing was left to chance. This assured customers a predictable quality of service and satisfaction in any Harper Shop throughout the world.

Martha's franchise model was not an act of charity, but a purposeful model designed to cost-efficiently expand a business while achieving her social objectives. She created a team of loyal, ambitious women who followed her precepts and business practices as if they were scriptures, and whom she and customers worldwide trusted to carry on the Harper tradition with consistency and finesse. She changed these women's lives and her own by creating this new business structure.

Firm expectations were placed on the shop owners. Franchisees had to purchase only Harper hair and skin products, including the shampoo, hair tonic and creams, that Martha manufactured; they were also updated on new procedures and products. Martha toured their shops periodically to assure that her standards were being upheld. National advertising campaigns were launched that encouraged shop participation. Ads were provided for franchisees to place in their local newspapers; seasonal specials often were promoted. Suggestions for creative promotions and marketing came from the home office. Signage was controlled.

Later, Harper franchises received a bimonthly and then monthly newsletter that updated franchisees on the latest methods and products and, of course, included an encouraging column from Martha to "her girls." A centralized system was created to place operators, mostly recent graduates but also those who needed a new job location. Similarly, a system to buy and sell Harper franchises was established. Benefits included group insurance, ongoing training and support, and the opportunity to attend "re-unions, periodic gatherings of Harper shop owners and operators, where they were updated on Harper techniques, introduced to new products, and generally inspired" (*Harper Method Progress* 1930, 16; *Harper Method Progress* 1938, 9, 11, 12).

Martha became the mother of American retail franchising by creating this business format. Her model did not become a dominant business force until the second half of the twentieth century, according to franchising expert Thomas Dicke. Coca-Cola did have its products sold in retail outlets in 1899, as did Rexall Drug in 1903, but neither of these duplicated small business operations as Martha's network of shops did. Eventually, Howard Johnson, McDonald's, Kentucky Fried Chicken, Domino's Pizza, and the many others re-created Martha's powerful model.

Ray Kroc, head of McDonald's, the personification of our present-day image of retail franchising, spoke about the potency of this entrepreneurial model when he declared, "Franchising has become an updated version of the American Dream" (Dicke 1992, 126). In the late 1960s, a pamphlet promoting franchising opportunities for black business owners pointedly stated it was a "guide for the people in the Black community who want economic as well as political rights" (T. Jones 1968, 1).

Nearly sixty years before, Martha Matilda Harper understood franchising's economic potential. While it seems unlikely that she knew the term "franchise" came originally from a French word meaning "free from servitude" (*Franchise Opportunities Handbook* 1994, ix), her new structure did just that. Her business expansion envisioned establishing servant girls as owners in Harper Shops throughout the world. She called these women "agents."

Martha also understood the importance of properly training her "girls," because once they left her shop, she had little direct control over their actions. Fifty years later, Dicke observed that franchises like Domino's Pizza nearly failed because they lacked effective training programs (1992, 131). Martha did not make that mistake; initially her training program was informally conducted at her Founder's Shop in Rochester. There trainees, depending on their pace of learning, might spend a few or many months, even years, learning the exacting science of the Harper Method. Eventually, in the 1920s, the Harper training function was separated from the shop and a formal school was created, just as McDonald's later created its Hamburger University.

Rachel Stothart, a Harper assistant, opened Detroit's first Harper Shop in 1891 and became the second Harper franchise owner.
Courtesy of Harper Method Progress.

The Harper franchise system required shop owners to buy Harper equipment—the custom-designed shampoo bowl, chair, and dryer—in addition to purchasing Harper products. As needed, Martha prefunded the opening of the shops and the Harperites paid off their debts as their business grew stronger. When those payments ended, Miss Corcoran, a Harper franchisee, remembered, "[the Harper Shop owner] felt she was on the highway to wealth" (*Harper Method Progress* Aug. 1930, 16).

That was just what Martha wanted. Her system changed the bleak future women faced. The first "branch office," as her franchises were called, was opened in Buffalo by her sister Harriet. Later it was owned by her niece Orpha (*Harper Method Progress* Aug. 1930, 14). According to *Golden Memories,* "In 1891, [Martha] sent Rachel Stothart to Detroit. To Chicago in 1893 went Mrs. Reynolds, later to be succeeded by Miss Farquhar, age 24" (1938, 12).

The same Mrs. Palmer who signed the petition to bring the Harper Shop to Chicago was honored at the Chicago World's Fair, and may have played a role in establishing a Harper Shop in Chicago for the Fair. Katherine Anthony established that Mrs. Palmer, President of the Board of Lady Managers of the Fair, was anxious for women to have an impact, and Susan B. Anthony was helping to focus attention on women (1975, 417). Harperite Betty Wheeler stated that, according to Harper lore, Susan B. Anthony specifically encouraged Martha to open the shop in time to take full advantage of this world exposure. Whether it was Mrs. Palmer or Susan B. Anthony, or both of them, Martha was helped by women supporting women.

As Martha's business began to bloom, the Robertses' affluence waned. We know few details except from various court depositions associated with the Robertses' estate battle. In testimony, Martha reported that in 1892, Mr. Roberts ran into financial problems; $30,000 of his money was lost in Staten Island real estate and other amounts were lost in unwise business investments. Martha rescued the Robertses' home and their assets; she paid $1500 in interest to protect the house (M. Harper 1933, 1702). She testified:

> When the crash came . . . I stepped forward and borrowed money to save [Mrs. Roberts's] property; and from that time on I [took care of] the bills, taxes, interest on mortgages to keep the home over their heads. . . . I . . . ran the house, took care of her; she was ill and had to go to the hospital and I paid all the hospital bills. . . . Then I had to borrow money from my friends. I paid 15% interest . . . to stave off the foreclosure. . . . I had a lot of very good friends among the girls. (M. Harper 1933, 1702)

That was the point at which the once wealthy Robertses became Martha's dependents.

As Martha's role changed, she faced more severe confrontations with Mr. Roberts and his attorney, Seward French, whom she removed at least twice from the premises because of his excessive drinking. That led to more harassment of Martha. She later testified, "It was while Mr. Roberts was associated with Seward French that he kept urging me to sign various papers" (M. Harper 1933, 1702). In fact, according to Martha's attorney, Frank Dinse, Martha was forced by a drunk Mr. Roberts to sign a February 12, 1894, agreement that gave Mrs. Roberts half the value of the Harper trademark and the Mascaro Tonique patent (F. Dinse 1933, 1702).

Decades passed before this document was produced, and according to Martha and Dinse, Mrs. Roberts never exercised that agreement. We lack much more detail. We do know that Martha never deserted Mrs. Roberts and that she continued to support both of the Robertses; however, Martha never honored that contract. Whether it was because she was "forced" to sign it or whether it was that she thought her lifetime support of the Robertses was sufficient, the Robertses were never part of her business ownership. Martha reserved that for herself and her "girls."

Martha and her partners (her "girls") had a mutual self-interest. The more Harper Shops flourished, the more demand there was for Harper products and trainees. The Harper operators, whose lives were transformed by Martha, grew in number and became independent wage earners. Martha's franchising system provided a revolutionary new business path for the success of both her Harperites and herself.

Curiously, Martha Matilda Harper and her role in creating franchising for a business and social objective are now forgotten, while Andrew Carnegie is better remembered for his philanthropy at the end of his life, when he gave away $300 million, rather than for his unethical business dealings. Carnegie biographer Harry Livesay suggested, "In giving [the millions] away, he found peace" (1975, 188). Libraries, churches, universities, the Carnegie Foundation, the Peace Palace at the Hague all benefited from his later life generosity.

Another business magnate of the time, John D. Rockefeller, provides a stark contrast to Martha's relationship with her franchise affiliates. While the name Rockefeller is still remembered and admired, the actual person lived in fear. As a result of his business tactics, Rockefeller felt compelled to install a home security system that would protect him from unwanted intrusion and potential attack. According to historian Stewart Holbrook, "[Rockefeller] wanted to live . . . unmolested by the many dangerous enemy incidents; no man with a bomb or a gun was to get into the old man's presence without effort" (1953, 343). In contrast, Martha's representatives were always welcome house guests; in fact, she bought a home with twenty-two rooms to accommodate her "girls."

Eventually, recognizing that his estate was "rolling up" and that he must do something with it, Rockefeller set up the Rockefeller Foundation "to advance the well-being of mankind throughout the world." By 1950, the Rockefeller Foundation had given away more than $800 million (Holbrook 1953, 344). Today, the Rockefeller Foundation is a prestigious and innovative charity.

Martha Matilda Harper made different decisions about her business goals; they influenced how she structured and ran her business as well as how she shared her wealth. To her, how a person behaved was part of the bigger statement to be made. From the start her franchise model suggested a new way of approaching business, with a goal of sharing opportunity and profits with needy women rather than maximizing her own gain. She believed in a win-win model where her business literally depended on the mutual success of her franchise owners and her parent business. Her style, based on her strong religious convictions, emphasized trust, kindness, cooperation, teamwork, and mutual support, fulfilled her need to be needed and to create a predictable environment that she could control, and from which she and others could make money.

Martha wanted to change the financial landscape for working-class women, and that meant using money to benefit them. She used her business to cause social change and provide economic power within her enterprise. While her own wealth grew, it was in direct proportion to the success of the Harper franchisees. MacMurchy wrote in *The Toronto,* "Desire for monopoly is entirely foreign to her character. It is a great happiness to her to have furnished so many women with a good employment, a good business into which they can put their own savings, and the profit of which is theirs. . . . Truly, Miss Harper is a remarkable woman; and she adds to modern business a grace, justice and freedom of her own" (1914, 20).

CHAPTER SIX

Expanding the Business

MARTHA UNDERSTOOD that recruiting the right women to carry on the Harper Method was essential to her business's successful growth. She taught shop owners about the importance of their operators. She preached in the *Harper Method Textbook,* "The reputation of your Shop depends upon [the Harper operator] as well as upon yourself. You want someone obviously well-bred and pleasant-looking. Not every girl is temperamentally fit. . . . It requires character, personality, health, intelligence, tact and poise" (1926, 184).

When Martha told her "girls" where to locate, they went. In addition to the initial three cities where she sent her trusted sister Harriet and assistants Rachel Stothart and Bertha Farquhar, others grasped opportunities in distant communities. Kate Sullivan trekked to St. Paul; Mrs. J. M. Small opened her shop in Starbuck, Washington; and Etta Nott located her shop in Janesville, Wisconsin. Closer to Rochester, Evelyn Selover went to Ithaca, and Janet Weir opened her shop in Pittsburgh. Across the country, Mrs. R. A. Shattuck pioneered in Spokane, Washington, and Louise Enger in San Francisco, and in the East, Julia DeLaney launched her business in Boston. Other urban centers and smaller communities, spanning the nation and crossing national borders, soon were touched by the Harper Method.

Customer demand continued to spur growth. Christian Scientists, suffragists, and the social and political elite were Martha's devoted fans. Out-of-town visitors continued to stimulate both interest and entry into other communities. When socially prominent St. Paul residents came to

Julia Delaney and her sister opened a
Harper Shop in Boston in 1908.
Courtesy of Harper Method Progress.

the Harper Shop in Chicago and experienced its services, they mobilized
and promised to patronize a Harper Shop located in their city. They also
promised Martha they would support any operator she chose. Kate
Sullivan was Martha's choice. Sullivan initially worked with Farquhar
and then, as St. Paul residents had requested, she opened a shop in their
city with great success (*Harper Method Progress* Sept. 1938, 5).

Such success was a matter of recruitment and training. The U.S.
Census occupational statistics, starting in 1870, listed a broad range of
jobs under "Domestic and Personal Services" in addition to domestics

and laundresses. They included garbage collectors and scavengers, fortune tellers, hypnotists, spiritualists, circus helpers, midwives, and nurses (not trained). Ironically for Harperites, barbers, hairdressers, and manicurists were still lumped with domestics.

However, there was a major difference between being a servant and being a hairdresser, especially a Harper operator. While the number of women servants remained large, the percentage of women who worked as servants declined from 47 percent in 1880 to 22 percent in 1930 (Meyerowitz 1988, 5). There were good reasons to leave domestic service.

For black women, becoming a Harperite was not a possibility until the mid-twentieth century. Domestic service was one of few job alternatives they had. As one black servant described her life in the early 1900s, she articulated why women wanted a different employment prospect: "Though today we are enjoying nominal freedom, we are literally slaves. . . . I frequently work fourteen to sixteen hours a day. . . . And what do I get for this work—this lifetime bondage? The pitiful sum of ten dollars a month! With this money I'm expected to pay my house rent . . . feed and clothe myself and three children" (Brownlee and Elliot 1976, 245–246).

Though white women faced gender bias in the workplace, they often were able to pursue jobs with somewhat greater career opportunities, higher pay, and more defined work hours. The majority of black women had fewer options. As late as the 1940s, estimates suggest that 60 percent of working black women were servants; they went from farms to households. It would take over a decade for black female entrepreneurs like Madam Walker and Annie Malone to provide these women with the alternative career opportunities Harper was offering.

Meanwhile, Martha targeted the women with whom she was familiar—white women trained as servants who sought something more for their lives. Martha and they recognized what Edward Shorters, a historian of the times, declared: "Economically independent women have greater liberty than economically dependent ones" (quoted in Meyerowitz 1988, xxi). The Harper Method provided a path to that liberty.

Having recruited these women into her operation, Martha became their crusading preacher, bridging their past experience to her vision of a more positive future. In an issue of the *Harper Method Progress,* she described those pioneers this way: "From a mere handful of women fighting public prejudice . . . they helped to found Harper Method in Truth and Principle and those qualities have been our guiding stars through [the] years" (Aug. 1930, 1). Emphasizing the importance of the individual, in the *Harper Method Textbook* Martha reminded the recruits of their critical role as Harper operators:

> [You are] the most important link in the Harper method chain. . . . [You] might be called the personification of Harper Service. . . . We are helping women attain the best that life has to offer—self-expression. . . . It is a vocation to be approached with humility . . . and above all, the love of service. It must be conducted with dignity, intelligence, and never-relaxing care. [You have not] . . . adopted the work primarily to make [your] living. [You are] . . . making . . . [your] living, by choice, through serving other women and thus the world about . . . [you]. (1926, 192)

With those words, Martha provided the compelling theme that guided these young white women as they broke out of their traditional roles and dared to become independent. She wooed them with a career prospect based on science and higher purpose.

Martha also persuaded them that her franchise system would lead to their financial freedom. This explains why Harper's first assistant, Bertha Farquhar, age twenty-four, bravely left her home and friends in Rochester, and traveled halfway across the country to Chicago in time to set up a Harper business to capitalize on the Chicago World's Fair. Farquhar later reflected in the newsletter, "It was a dubious and little known profession. . . . [Yet, she recalled it was] . . . enthusiasm and loyalty to her employer [which] . . . caused her to pioneer"(*Harper Method Progress* July–Aug. 1932, 26). Soon she relocated to the prestigious and popular Marshall Field's building and department store, conveniently located for easy access to customers for shopping and transportation home via streetcars.

Demand for the services of the day, shampooing and brushing, grew quickly. Even though customers resented her fine comb—associating it with lice treatment—Farquhar recalled that Martha persisted because it was an essential part of the cleaning process. There were no shortcuts in the Harper Method. As the shops' popularity grew, more products were manufactured and stored in the Powers Building and the Robertses' shed, and more assistants and franchisees were needed to extend the reach of the Harper experience.

Martha recruited carefully, and conveyed a sense of personal accountability, if not of guilt, to each woman who became a Harperite. She made it clear to the newcomers that they were being entrusted with her name and reputation, which were to be treated as precious gems. Each operator was responsible for the reputation of the Harper franchise system Martha was building. Martha understood that she needed to create a passionate group of followers, far from the home office, in order to successfully expand her franchise system. Without total compliance, she could not assure the consistency of quality and service, the key factors in determining the effectiveness of the system.

Martha further galvanized her women into a cohesive group by identifying their accomplishments as women. Suggesting that men would not place their names on a franchise operation, in the *Harper Method Textbook* she contrasted that reluctance with the situation of herself and her "girls," reminding them of their opportunity and responsibility (1926, 30). Her language and entire system suggest a purposeful, charismatic business, not unlike today's direct selling organizations of Avon and Mary Kay Cosmetics. Like those organizations, Martha provided a path for ambitious women who traditionally had been denied a slice of the economic opportunity pie. She needed committed believers and she gave them a cause—the economic rights of women.

Timing was key. The industry, in its infancy, was still being defined and had not yet excluded women from leadership. It provided a nonconfrontational opportunity ideal for former servants, like Martha and her recruits, to seize. The roles Martha carved out built on ladylike behavior; by associating with upper-class customers, the Harperites' status was implicitly raised, just as their commitment to provide healthful service elevated their need and right to work. They were told, and came to believe, that they were not money-grubbing women, but devoted practitioners breaking down gender stereotypes by judiciously forming a worthy organization and working in a worthy profession.

Women brave enough to try this new beauty concept entered a shop that sparkled with cleanliness. Inside, decorum was firmly established. Harper trainees were taught that there was to be no discourtesy nor favoritism, and absolutely no gossiping about either customers or staff. Within a Harper Shop there was dignity and privacy. Martha strictly instructed her owners in the *Harper Method Textbook:*

> Never permit gossip. . . . [Do not] . . . indulge in this self-degrading vice, either among [yourselves] or with [your] patrons. Some women, it is true, seem to enjoy publishing unpleasant personal anecdotes wherever they may be, but yours is a Harper Method Shop and its attitude should be one of dignity and refinement. The better class of clientele . . . is immediately prejudiced against a headquarters for gossip. One gossipy attendant can give an evil name to a Shop otherwise superbly conducted. (1926, 182)

Just as customer satisfaction attracted more patrons, so recruits came by word of mouth from satisfied operators and owners. Once one family member came, it was not unusual for others to follow. Martha began with her family, attracting sisters (Emma and Harriet), then nieces (Orpha, Ann, and Nell). Rachel Stothart set up one of the earliest franchises in Detroit. Her relative Mina was recruited by Martha. Mina described how it happened in the *Harper Method Progress:*

> I was a young, unsophisticated country girl. [Martha's] charming personality and kindly interest easily decided me when she suggested I take up her work. . . . I spent one and a half years in training . . . [Martha] taught me many things, not only the actual work but the pleasant manner in which she met and greeted her patrons . . . Our training meant good hard work and Miss Harper shared . . . the long days with us. . . . We began at 8AM, lunched any time and kept open one night a week for business girls until 10 PM. A lunch was supplied that night, and what a happy time we had. Our teacups were turned up, and one of the girls told our fortunes. One of two things was to be our fate. We were either to marry a very rich man or to have a wonderful Harper Method shop. (Aug. 1930, 7)

In 1905 Mina Stothart created a Harper Shop in New York City. By 1938, she was Mrs. Ramsdell, and her Harper Salon was located on Fifth Avenue. *Courtesy of* Golden Memories.

To Martha and many of those early pioneers, marriage was not an attractive alternative. For many reasons, some linked to her traumatized childhood, Martha consciously created a sense of family within her business. Shop owners were encouraged to visit Rochester and stay with her in the Robertses' house. To Martha, her "girls" were daughters. To Mrs. Roberts, they were unwelcome intruders. As a customer and friend, Mrs. Force, recalled: "When Mrs. Roberts was with Harper agents, especially representatives from Chicago [it was clear she] did not want them in the house and did not want to entertain them. Mrs. Roberts was only interested in her dog, fish and birds" (Force 1933, 1702).

Another story about Mrs. Roberts illustrates how Martha operated. According to testimony of Martha's niece, Ann Harper, she paid Mrs. Roberts $10 a week to stay in her home, at Martha's suggestion, because when she first came, she overhead Mrs. Roberts emphatically tell her Aunt Martha, "I do not want another member of the family here. I do not want [Ann] in this house" (1933, 1702). Yet, per Martha's directions, Mrs. Roberts was never left alone, and often Ann or others stayed to care for her. That was Martha's way; she was unflappable, with an empathetic temperament, loyalty, and a focus on the bigger picture. She brought others along.

Martha's determined but gentle nature is recorded by many. Martha seemed to instill self-confidence in others by allowing them to err. Her teaching style was interesting; she demanded total compliance with *her* methods, yet she provided her students with the opportunity to fail in safe situations. In the *Harper Method Progress,* Mary Nelson, who opened Harper Shops in Hartford and Denver, recalled:

> While I was in training . . . I had given a shampoo and discovered I had
> the lady's hair so badly tangled that I did not know what was going to
> happen. . . . Miss Harper's watchful eyes [saw the situation]. She left the
> lady she was working on, came over to me and said, "Miss Nelson,
> suppose we exchange customers for a while." She got all the tangles out,
> and the lady never knew anything had gone wrong. Miss Harper never
> gave me one word of reproach but when I tried to apologize, said it was
> quite all right, I would know better next time. It was a little thing, but
> it meant much to me and I never forgot her kindness and tact. (Aug.
> 1930, 19)

As the need grew for Harper operators and franchisees, women traveled significant distances to learn the Harper Method (Mary Nelson
came from New York City). They needed to live somewhere safe in
Rochester while training. They were joined by other working women
who were moving away from home or live-in positions, choosing to
become what Joanne Meyerowitz called "women adrift."

In Rochester, with its strong immigrant flow and its booming indus
trial and service sectors, 20 percent of women workers were lodgers in
1900 (Meyerowitz 1988, 4). Some lived at organized residences like the
YWCAs, which many independent young women resented for the charitable tinge and for the control over their hours, their makeup, and their
food. As Theodore Dreiser had his heroine Sister Carrie exclaim, "I will
not go home! I will *not* be good! I will *not* reform!" (quoted in
Meyerowitz 1988, 117). This push for greater independence, away from
well-meaning, but controlling women, reinforced for the Harper women
the unique opportunity that Harper affiliation offered.

While they were joining the Harper sisterhood, the environment
around these women was changing in the 1890s. Two industries were
undergoing dramatic changes. The world of fashion, once controlled by
custom dressmakers and designers, was having to compete with department stores and wholesale garment makers that separated production
from direct sales. The result, according to Wendy Gamber, was "a gender transformation of the field of fashion" (1997, 188–189). Men began to dominate the fashion industry, and after 1930 they controlled it.
Ironically, this industrial transformation enabled working-class women

to look more "fashionable," at the cost of the entrepreneurial success of their sister dressmakers and milliners.

As this was occurring, the beauty industry emerged. In the 1890s, as cities began to electrify, people started seeing each other more clearly and increasingly accepted the concept of being looked at, even photographed. Yet change came slowly. According to Mary Anderson, author of the U.S. government's report on the beauty field, *Inside the Doors of Beauty Shops*, "Before 1920 [beauty shops] were little known" (1935, 1).

Before this era Martha and her "girls" quietly appeared and strategically captured a niche in this evolving beauty market. Building on Martha's charm, determination, religious principles, and timely expertise, the Harper Method took off, espousing principles of health and beauty that went below the surface. As described in the *Harper Method Textbook*, the role of the operator was to bring out the natural beauty of the customer: "A healthy woman exhibits allurement which we call . . . beauty" (1926, 12).

Each Harper shop was a refuge: immaculate, orderly, full only of Harper products, and offering extraordinary and painstaking service. Looking almost like a hospital room, with operators dressed in white uniforms, aprons, and white hats like nurses' caps, it had an antiseptic feeling. Upon entering the shop, a woman brave enough to try this new beauty concept was reassured that she was in professional hands.

Martha's salons became havens for refreshment, since Harper shampoos included a head and shoulder massage to stimulate blood flow. Facials intended to be both restful and stimulating, were offered. Martha instructed her Harperites in the *Harper Method Textbook* that they themselves had to be "peaceful and happy" (1926, 131) in order to induce similar feelings in their customers.

The *Harper Method Textbook* taught that the Harper facial did not concentrate solely on the face, but included the shoulders, the back, the neck, and the head, all to be caressed and stimulated with specific motions and creams. It began with a circular massage of the chest, chin, and neck, followed by the "saddle maneuver," which stimulated the area around the shoulder and then awakened the skin toward the spine. Next came the "strapping action," in which a Harperite's hand swept across one of the customer's shoulders and briskly awoke the skin across the back before the operator's hand reached the customer's other shoulder.

Then, using a "chucking motion," the operator's fingers rapidly stimulated the customer's lower face, starting at the chin. Next "peach movements" were used; the balls of the fingers stimulated the area around the mouth. Then, using a rotary motion, the operator's hands massaged the area from the chin to the temples. The nose and eye areas were then stimulated. The "pit-pat" motion of the operator's fingers crossed the chest three times. Then the operator's hands fluttered across the customer's entire face, one hand revolving around the other in a gentle tapping motion.

Throughout the process, motions were reversed to balance the effect, but all went upward and outward, with the operator's fingers directing the blood flow away from the heart and tightening the skin. A mask was applied, and warm and cold towels relaxed and awakened the customer's shoulder, head, and facial muscles (*Harper Method Textbook* 1926, 134–141). After nearly two hours of such treatment, each customer felt rejuvenated, pampered, and very relaxed, with glowing skin and a calm disposition.

Martha's commitment to mindfulness, good health, and kindly interaction among people reflected how Christian Science continued to influence her business dealings and philosophy. Locally, the group of Christian Science practitioners grew, and by 1897 members were no longer meeting in parlors, but had moved into the Triangle Building. That was the year, according to membership records, when Martha Matilda Harper officially joined the local church. In April 1897 she became the 121st member of the First Church of Christ, Scientist, Rochester. Those church records also suggest that Martha recruited Mrs. Roberts, because sometime between 1899 and 1906, she joined the church.

Despite critics lambasting Eddy and her followers for attracting "frustrated women eager to satisfy their craving for dominance in a larger society," the religion grew dramatically between the early 1890s and 1910 (Peel 1988, 94, 110). Other successful entrepreneurs, such as Alfred C. Fuller, the founder of the Fuller Brush Company, also were drawn to Mrs. Eddy's teachings and became practitioners. While Fuller personally did not incorporate the commitment to equality in business as he led his Fuller Brush *men* to greater earnings, he, like other entrepreneurs, shared with Martha the self-confidence to pursue an innovative business approach.

Perhaps these entrepreneurs were attracted to Christian Science's belief in their individual power to connect with God and to reduce both personal and work-induced pain ranging from spiritual needs to monetary concerns. Christian Science writer Robert Peel acknowledges, "Christian Science . . . grew up in a business culture and since its mission embraced the healing of disabilities and difficulties of every kind, this naturally included business and financial problems" (1988, 27).

As the twentieth century neared, developments in hair technology dramatically affected the industry, but not Martha. A number of men applied their inventiveness to this field. In 1897, a Frenchman named Marcel Grateau created a curling iron, known as the marcel iron, through a serendipitous error. By using a curling iron upside down, he discovered the "marcel wave" and it became the rage. According to historian Lois W. Banner, Charles Nessler invented the first permanent waving machine in 1906; in the early days, it took up to ten hours to complete the wave. In 1915 he began manufacturing the machine and related supplies, although it did not become popular until the 1920s, when artificial hair was no longer widely used. In the United States, Alexandre Godefroy invented the hot blast hair dryer, which was too costly and large for home use (Banner 1983, 39, 215).

Women were also seizing opportunities available to them in this new beauty industry. Between 1890 and 1924, over 450 trademarks for beauty preparations were filed by women. Martha, meanwhile, was trying to maintain the focus on her core competencies of healthful hair treatments rather than short-lived hair styles or procedures like permanents or marceling. It proved to be a fundamental dividing line between her and the profit-seeking industry.

The *Harper Method Textbook* directed the operator to "allow the patron to 'do' her own hair after a shampoo or treatment." Martha's explanation was that "This practice frees the time of the Operator for . . . more important work and avoids the risk of failing to please in dressing the patron's hair. Dressing the hair for special occasions is a convenience offered to those who wish it and should never be developed at the expense of other and more important branches of your work" (1926, 88).

Despite these radical views, the Harper network grew dramatically, with each shop's success supporting the next one while Martha orchestrated the expansion process. The stories of these early Harperites underscore how effectively Martha had formed her cohesive, self-protective group. While individuality was clearly expressed, a sense of group identity propelled and protected members.

At Martha's direction, Ena Boscoe Premus opened a Harper Shop in San Francisco in 1903. According to Ena, the move made her lonely and sad because she had spent four years in Rochester at the Training School and shop. When she left for the West Coast, she targeted wealthy San Franciscans, who became her customers and supported her growth. As a result, she added four operators. Then came the devastating 1906 earthquake, and she lost everything.

Crediting the support of other Harper offices, she managed to reopen. However, "After two years, I married, sold my office and was away . . . for eight years. Financial reverses forced me into business again and by working hard I have built up a good business where I now keep five operators busy all the time" (*Harper Method Progress* Aug. 1930, 6). Such publicized experiences spoke of how supportive the Harper network was of the individual, the strength of the Harper franchise to endure through financial or natural disasters, and the profitability and durability of Harper franchised ownership.

Other tales documented the spread of the Harper Shops in 1905 to Toronto and New York City. Jennie Cameron, a Harper franchisee, was credited with "Harperizing the King's Dominions" (*Harper Method Progress* Aug. 1930, 23). Cameron recalled that it was a hot July night when Miss Harper drove her, in a pony-drawn buggy, to Charlotte to catch a steamer bound for Kingston. After she arrived in Toronto's Union Station, Cameron trudged from building to building, looking for office space. After three days she was successful, and the Harper Method was launched in Toronto. Six months later she fell on the ice and fractured her left wrist.

What happened next reflects the security and support the Harper franchise system offered franchisees: "Having unbounded faith in Miss Harper's interest to help her family along, I wired her for assistance, as there was no one in Canada whom I could call to my aid. Three hours later [Miss Harper] had an assistant on the train coming to my rescue" (*Harper Method Progress* Aug. 1930, 23). From that point on, the Toronto shop prospered, and some of its shop operators went on to open other shops throughout Canada. The message was clear: You were not alone when you were a Harperite.

That same year, Mina Stothart opened a New York City branch, and her recollections illustrate the devotion these Harper women felt for Martha and their clear understanding of how it affected them as women.

> We started for the big city with . . . determination (which no one thought I had).

> At last our first customer entered. She was sent by Miss Farquhar of Chicago. Such joy! We used and sold [Harper preparations only] . . . and we experienced the fruit of our labor, for, "once a Harper patron, always one."

> Let [Miss Harper's] heart rejoice, knowing her girls love her and appreciate what she has done for womanhood. (*Harper Method Progress* Aug. 1930, 7-8)

Martha, just as she wanted, became the titular and emotional leader of the Harper force. Harperites believed they owed her their success, and they devotedly followed her. Harperite Minnie Corcoran, who at the turn of the century ran a shop in York, Pennsylvania, for five years, reported that Martha suggested she open another shop in Baltimore. While they were working toward that goal, the 1908 Baltimore fire occurred, leveling the city. As the two of them toured the city, Corcoran reported, "My courage left me and I was for postponing the venture for a year or two. But Miss Harper with her almost uncanny judgment replied, 'No, now is the time to do it; the city is flattened and confused;

grow up with it, and about in this spot is the place to do it' " (*Harper Method Progress* Aug. 1930, 15). Six months later, exactly in that spot, Minnie Corcoran opened her successful shop. This entrepreneurial duo did not stop. In 1913 they opened another shop in Providence, Rhode Island.

Rebecca Nichols recalled how, when she opened a shop in Cincinnati in 1908, she capitalized on both illness and the needs of working women.

> To us fell the task of educating women to the necessity of giving their hair systematic, scientific treatment in a modernly equipped shop. . . . We worked cheap in those days. . . . I gave a shampoo treatment and round curl for seventy five cents. Teachers and business girls were given three treatments for one dollar. . . . A few cases of typhoid fever and severe illness where the hair had fallen out and been replaced by a strong glossy growth through Harper Method treatments were a great help in building up a steady trade. (*Harper Method Progress* Aug. 1930, 10)

As Americans who patronized Harper Shops traveled abroad, they found Harper Method Shops awaiting them. Europeans became enamored, and even national leaders acknowledged Martha. Emma Burgeleit, an early Harperite, recalled that when she and her sister set up the Berlin shop in 1909, "Miss Harper visited us in Berlin shortly after we were located. . . .We had so many interesting people as patrons—people from all over the globe. . . . In 1913, Miss Harper paid us another visit. . . . the former Kaiser [Wilhelm saluted] her on one of our walks (*Harper Method Progress* Sept. 1938, 9) . . . as he passed her in his car with the King of England, the Czar of Russia and the King of Italy" (*Harper Method Progress* Sept. 1938, 5).

According to MacMurchy's newspaper article, after operating for over a quarter of a century, Martha had over 134 franchises in 128 cities in Canada, the United States, England, Scotland, France, and Germany. A shop was being established in Rome, and requests from all over the world, including China, were reviewed (1914, 20).

During these years, the early 1900s, newcomers named Madam Sarah Walker, Helena Rubinstein, Elizabeth Arden, and Annie Malone were building their beauty businesses. The industry provided the two determined black women (Walker and Malone) entrepreneurial outlets for themselves and their black sisters; they seized that opportunity with a

Martha Harper (*right*) with E. Seibel and Emma
Burgeleit, sisters, while visiting her German
franchise in 1913. In 1909, Martha helped the
sisters open the Harper Shop in Berlin. Prior to
World War I, the sisters left the country and
established shops on the West Coast in America.
Courtesy of Harper Method Progress.

passion and values similar to Martha's. George Schuyler, a columnist for
the *Messenger*, referred to Madam Walker as "A Race Wonder Woman
who had emancipated her sisters from economic and psychological slavery" (quoted in Peiss 1998, 209).

Madam Walker was a self-made black millionaire, born Sarah Breedlove
in 1867 in Delta, Louisiana, the daughter of former slaves; her story

parallels Martha's in many ways. Martha was bound out at seven; Breedlove was orphaned at that age. Breedlove married at fourteen, to get a roof over her head, and was widowed at twenty with a daughter, A'Lelia. Like Martha, Breedlove survived by doing what was necessary; she washed clothes. She was introduced to the black cosmetics business through her side job of selling cosmetics for Annie Malone, another black female in the beauty business.

Martha's business opportunity came about while working for a physician; Breedlove worked as a cook for a pharmacist, E. L. Scholtz. There she experimented with various hair conditioners, shampoos, and oils to help her own hair, which was falling out. Based on her accomplishments, she launched a beauty business targeted to African-American women. She married a former newspaper salesman, C. J. Walker, and took the name Madam Walker ("The National Business Hall of Fame" 1992, 6–7).

With a commitment to service similar to what the Harper Method professed, Madam Walker's business was founded on the principle of providing "unselfish service and a full measure of quality and quantity" (*Madam C. J. Walker Beauty Manual* n.d., 20). Her business prospered, and according to Walker literature, her women could earn as much as $23 a week (versus the $2 a week they might make as maids in the South). Like Martha, Madam Walker employed a tutor and took courses to improve herself as her business grew. She ultimately divorced her husband, but C. J. remained a Walker agent for the rest of his life ("The National Business Hall of Fame" 1997, 7; *Madam C. J. Walker Beauty Manual* n.d., 16).

Both Martha and Walker recognized the struggle women faced to succeed, and Walker urged them to find strength within themselves, stating in the *Madam C. J. Walker Beauty Manual:* "It is within one's own self to weave that cloth that clothes one's future and makes one a success or failure in proportion to her faith in God and her faith in her own abilities" (n.d., foreword).

Even as the first black woman entrepreneur who became a self-made millionaire, Walker faced the societal prejudice most such women in that era experienced because of their gender. At a 1912 convention of the National Negro Business League, the session chairman, Booker T. Washington, refused to recognize her. Jumping to her feet, she declared,

> Surely you are not going to shut the door in my face, ...I am a woman who came from the cotton fields of the South. I was promoted from there to the washtub and then to the kitchen. Then I promoted myself into the business of manufacturing hair goods, and I built my own factory on my own ground. My object in life is not simply to make money for myself. I use part of what I make in trying to help others. (quoted in "The National Business Hall of Fame" 1997, 7)

Annie Malone, Madam Walker's mentor, was born Annie Turnbo in 1869, and she, too, was orphaned as a child. Living with her siblings in Illinois, she eventually experimented with a variety of herbs to help the skin and hair problems plaguing many black women. By 1900 she had developed a hair treatment based on folk tradition. With her sister, she relocated to the black community of Lovejoy, Illinois, and manufactured a proprietary hair growth product. Going door-to-door, she persuaded the skeptical residents that her treatment was effective. In 1902 she moved to St. Louis, which had a large black community, and extended her sales to the South and then nationwide. When she married Aaron Malone in 1914, her business was thriving.

Like Martha, Annie tried to inspire devotion to her business among her associates. Her business took on an evangelical ring as she called her sales force "evangels of Poro." In 1918, Malone opened Poro College, which contained her factory and offices, and "offered theatre, music, athletics, lectures, chapel services, and art murals. Reaching out to young women in need of training and jobs, Malone gave them—and black St. Louis—a wider view of culture" (Peiss 1998, 93).

Malone and Walker, like Martha, held strong spiritual beliefs and were determined to change the economic realities of people they cared about—their black sisters. Though their business models differed from Harper's, Walker shared her profits with her agents and her community, and Malone invested to better the lives of her employees and community. Harper's operation shared with Malone's and Walker's businesses a foundation based on a strong religious commitment, homeopathic knowledge, and entrepreneurial savvy rooted in missionary zeal. Each used her business to impact the society she hoped to improve. Malone and Walker refused to produce products like hair straighteners and bleaches that pandered to society's view that African-American's physical characteristics needed to be changed.

Though Walker and Malone had common childhood and economic hardships similar to Martha's and held a similar commitment to their sisters, their race separated them from Martha and they were never her competitors nor colleagues. It was Rubinstein and Arden who shared the white women's market with Martha.

Neither Rubinstein nor Arden was particularly concerned that her business should change the economic realities of her sisters. Their passions were themselves. Their business outlook was captured by Rubinstein's statement in Patrick O'Higgins's biography of her: "I am a firm believer in the saying, 'God helps those who help themselves' " (1971, 17). It was an approach more aligned with our traditional view of a business magnate—one who enjoys running the business for the sake of the process.

Elizabeth Arden was born Florence Nightingale Graham in a small Canadian village near Toronto in the late 1800s. Like Harper, Malone, and Walker, she lost her mother at an early age—five years. At thirty years of age, she followed her brother to New York City.

Like Martha, Arden was attracted to the beauty industry. From a clerical job with beautician Eleanor Adair, Arden worked her way up, learning how to give facials, then a popular beauty treatment. Before long she recognized, as Martha did, that to have money and social respect, she needed to run her own business. In 1909, Arden teamed up with Elizabeth Hubbard, who made and sold beauty products. Within a year that partnership dissolved, and Arden, then thirty-two—in contrast to Martha, Malone, or Walker—obtained a loan of several thousand dollars from her brother. With that money she opened her own shop on Fifth Avenue and created a new name for herself, Elizabeth

Arden. She thought the name was much more appropriate for the image and venture she was about to build.

Like the other beauty moguls, Helena Rubenstein understood that for a woman marriage had to be secondary to establishing a business. In 1908, she married in England, at the age of thirty-eight, after she had established a beauty business in Australia and opened her fashionable London salon with $100,000 of her Australian profits. In 1915, with a world war impending, she and her family fled to the United States, where she opened a chic shop in New York City and, two years later, one in San Francisco.

Born in Poland on December 25, 1870, Rubinstein was the eldest of eight sisters, many of whom later worked in her business. Raised by both parents and relatively well educated, she attended the University of Cracow and medical school in Switzerland before immigrating to Australia to join an uncle in 1902.

Though only four feet, ten inches tall, she had an elegant look that she cultivated in the rough land of Australia. She used her skin the way Martha used her long hair. Rubinstein's beautiful skin attracted attention from the sun-baked Australian women. Rubinstein obtained a loan and opened a small shop in Melbourne to sell her Creme Valaze. Like Martha, Rubinstein capitalized on praise from prominent women, recognizing the marketing impact of publicity and the income potential of selling to the upper-class market.

Though these beauty moguls—Martha Matilda Harper, Madam Walker, Annie Turnbo Malone, Elizabeth Arden, and Helena Rubinstein— expanded their businesses differently, they shared gender-based realities. None of these powerful women started her business before she was thirty. Each business was made possible by a creative mind exploiting an opportunity, a formula, a product, a prototype. The beauty industry provided this fresh environment. Seizing her opportunity, each broke from the traditional female mold and built an independent financial future.

Marriage, except for Madam Walker's teenage refuge, was postponed until each woman's priority—her business—was firmly established. Madam

Walker, Annie Malone, and Martha Matilda Harper wanted to change economic options for women; Arden and Rubinstein believed others could follow their successful paths. What bridges Harper to Walker and Malone is their spiritual connection, their poverty, and their determination to use their business success to change women's lives. Arden and Rubinstein, though not well-to-do, did have access to family money that enabled them to launch their businesses; Harper, Malone, and Walker literally had to save pennies to launch their enterprises (Purdy 1995, 2; Candee 1957, 20).

The impact of their cumulative efforts was to transform an industry; they blazed a new path for women as consumers and workers, redefining social mores and opportunity. Peiss concludes: "These businesswomen fashioned, in effect, a consumer market for beauty largely outside dominant distribution networks and the emerging organizations of national advertising and marketing. . . . Poor, working-class, and black women, largely ignored by national advertisers and magazines, joined the affluent in the market for beauty" (1998, 95).

Martha recognized the growing market and the competition, and responded either naively or brilliantly. In the *Harper Method Textbook* she urged her Harperites to focus on doing what they did best, delivering her system well. "The Harper Method has many contemporaries but it has no competitors" (1926, 3).

In *Barbara Burke's Beauty Journal,* an industry publication, Martha pointedly reminded all readers where to focus their energies. "Attention begins at home. Watching competitors is never so profitable, financially or morally, as watching your own shop, to see that it gives the highest service possible to every patron. Checking every detail of one's own shop work will absorb so much time and energy there will be no profit . . . or need [for the owners] . . . to worry about competitors" (Nov. 1929, 46).

These were exciting but exhausting times for Martha. She was turning her franchise system into an international operation; she was gaining wealth, and so were her franchisees; but she still had to cope with the Robertses. Mr. Roberts had declared bankruptcy in 1901, and his drinking continued. According to Martha, he insisted that she sign another agreement; this one agreed to share the profits of her business with the

Robertses in exchange for using their home to manufacture Harper products. Mrs. Roberts told her not to sign, but, for continued "peace in the household," Martha later testified, she signed, expecting nothing to come of it because she was paying all the Robertses' household and living expenses. To Martha's surprise, Mr. Roberts filed the March 31, 1908, agreement in the Monroe County Clerk's Office on August 16, 1909. He died on January 20, 1910. During this period the mortgage, still in Mrs. Robert's name, was paid by Martha. She placed a lien on the building for the amount of her payments. It was a messy affair.

Martha needed trusted help. In 1909 she hired John Bushfield, possibly a relative of a Geneva franchise owner, to help manage the business. He was a chemist and took over administrative duties, allowing her to travel more, monitoring and establishing new shops (Bushfield 1933). In 1912 she recruited her niece, Ann Harper, to manage the Harper Hairdressing Parlor in the Powers Building. Ultimately, Ann became the supervisor of the Harper Method School.

As a Christian Scientist, Martha had very specific beliefs about how her Harper ideal should be achieved through proper motivation and support. She encouraged her shop owners to practice an enlightened management style, suggesting they become the role model for their staff. In the *Harper Method Textbook* she urged Harper franchisees to systematically listen to their people, involve them, and make them feel like part of a Harper team. She told them to meet often with all operators, suggesting twenty minutes a session, to share ideas and criticism, because "They will assure—a unity of . . . purpose that will preserve the personality of your Shop. . . . The Owner can express a short general thought . . . as well as ideas on solving the problems that arise from day to day. Undesirable tendencies can be corrected (of course without mentioning names or causing offense), and gratifying accomplishments can be held up as praiseworthy examples" (1926, 182–83).

Martha knew it was time for a break, to refresh herself, to celebrate what had been accomplished, and to figure out what needed to be done. She needed to leave Rochester and Mrs. Roberts. It was time to take care of Martha.

CHAPTER  SEVEN

Pursuing Robert,
for Business and Pleasure

IN 1912, AT THE AGE OF FIFTY-FIVE, Martha Matilda Harper decided it was time for a real vacation. Accompanied by some of her devoted early shop owners, including Bertha Farquhar from Chicago and a Miss Pickett from Portland, she arranged for an extraordinary trek—a trip across the country leading to a five-day escorted jaunt through Yellowstone, America's first national park.

Many others—including the old, established families and nouveau riche tourists who came by train, stayed at park hotels, and toured the alluring terrain in stagecoaches—shared this momentous grand tour. They were adventurers of varying degrees, taking on the wilderness in style.

Yellowstone historian Aubrey Haines tells us that the majority of train travelers came via the Northern Pacific Railroad to the Gardiner terminus. Following that route, Martha and her group likely passed through the grasslands, then through Minnesota and the Dakota and Montana badlands, where the lonely vastness was briefly interrupted by isolated, tiny towns. They left the main line at Gardiner, a smaller town even than Livingston, Montana, about which Rudyard Kipling commented that he "exhausted the town 'including the saloons' in ten minutes" (Haines 1977, 102).

For $40 per person Martha and her companions were entitled to the five-day tour—all transportation, lodging, and meals. Dressed in linen dusters and bonnets, they transferred from the train to a stagecoach for

Bertha Farquhar, looking
the part of a successful
businesswoman, as she
operated her Chicago Harper
franchise in 1906. When
she died in 1932, she willed
the shop to two of her
most senior operators.
Courtesy of
Harper Method Progress.

the eight-mile ride to the National
Hotel at Mammoth Hot Springs.
Upon arrival, they became part of a
diverse crowd of businessmen, fron-
tiersmen, smartly dressed women, and
sportswomen with cameras. Their
schedule usually allowed for an afternoon of relaxation, and the group
might settle on the veranda to marvel
at the sights soon to be seen, or visit
nearby stores to purchase souvenir
spoons or postcards. The bolder tourists went to the hot spring terraces,
often with a hotel porter who acted
as their guide. Soldiers dressed in blue
uniforms provided a sense of security
against periodic holdups.

On the morning of the second day,
the grand tour went into full gear.
While the Harper women were eat-
ing breakfast, a parade of Yellowstone
Park Transportation Company stagecoaches lined up in front of the National Hotel. The drivers were young
cowboys or ranchmen who were paid
$50 a month. They worked during
the summers to supplement their in-
comes or simply to be part of the
open, carefree life. Often weather-
beaten or tobacco-stained, these men
looked aged beyond their years. They
retained a youthful spirit, however,
and often possessed exceptional
storytelling skill and an extroverted

nature that made them memorable characters, and certainly entertaining guides. Some of them were even good drivers. The guides included Geyser Bob, a teller of tales; Big Fred, a 320-pound giant of a man; and Society Red, who took in every dance he could (Haines 1977, 105, 107, 108, 122). Among these rough and tough hombres was a gentler, smaller man searching for a different future. He was Robert Arthur MacBain, Martha's future husband.

Like Martha, life had not been easy for him. Robert took six years to graduate from Simpson College in Indianola, Iowa, earning his keep along the way. His family, from the small farming community of Corning, Iowa, was consumed with farm life and put little value on "book learning." Their priority was productive farmwork that could be seen and marketed. Years later Robert poignantly described to his sister-in-law Lois MacBain that as a child, he, like Martha, felt like an outcast, although for different reasons: "I realized that my natural inclinations were never much in the direction of farm and country life. That alone sort of set me apart as a sour apple in the family tree" (R. MacBain 1964).

In 1910, at the age of twenty-nine, Robert, degree in hand, was proud of himself and full of optimism about his future, although he was unclear about his direction. After graduation, he followed the lure of the frontier and went west to the state of Washington; in 1911 he taught science in a high school. A letter from his mother on June 30, 1912, indicates that Robert headed to Yellowstone National Park during the summer because he hated teaching and was looking for something else to do (E. MacBain 1912, 2). It turned out to be a serendipitous decision.

The Harper women were assigned to the yellow stagecoach driven by handsome, thirty-one-year-old Robert MacBain. With his long face, piercing blue eyes, and slicked-back hair, he looked like a "dude" (slang for a tourist), rather than a "savage," as the drivers were called. At five-feet-nine, he must have towered over Martha Matilda Harper.

Robert MacBain took seriously the responsibility of maneuvering the four-horse, eleven-person stagecoach over rugged terrain, taking steep hills despite limited braking power. But he was first and foremost a charmer. He also was a quick study, and he knew how to play a role. As he gallantly helped the Harper women aboard, the cavalcade of coaches began to depart. Martha Matilda Harper the businesswoman no longer had to direct the course; she could sit back and enjoy the ride as Robert called out, "Gid'ap you Pirates!" and his whip stirred the horses to move (Haines 1977, 101, 107).

Periodically thoughts of her business and its enormous growth potential probably disrupted Martha's calm. She needed a new manufacturing plant. She wanted to get her products into department stores. How would it all happen? To take her business to the next level, Martha could not continue to do everything: recruit, motivate the staff, identify new sites and product needs—and worry about day-to-day operations. Putting those troubling thoughts aside, she likely turned her attention back to her charismatic driver and the natural beauty surrounding her.

Robert entertained his coach passengers with impeccable mimicry of immigrant tongues, especially those of his Scottish ancestors. Years later, Robert Dinse, a family friend, described Robert thus: "[He] was a true romantic. He knew he was. He was a charmer from the word go and he pushed it. He was . . . a raconteur. He loved to expand on stories. I haven't found anyone quite like him since. . . . I miss him" (R. Dinse 1995).

Depending on their driver for information and entertainment, the Harper women delighted in their good fortune to have such a bewitching storyteller. On they drove, past the narrow gorge called Golden Gate, past the Rustic Falls, Swan Lake Flat, across Garner River to Appolinaris Spring, where they stretched their legs and drank some water. Aboard the coach again, they passed Obsidian Cliff, where Indians had gathered the stone for arrowheads, and then Frying Pan Spring, where gas bubbled through the water. On they went to Larry's for lunch. Haines quoted one passenger who described it as a circus: "Everyone was jolly and hungry . . . a funny Irishman & the general manager, kept everyone in a [good mood]. It is fun to get away from the conventional big hotel" (1977, 110).

Then they proceeded to Norris Geyser Basin, where they walked along a boardwalk with the help of Robert. After riding over the dusty road and visiting Gibbon Falls, they were likely dead-tired and quite thirsty. Because hotel and restaurant proprietors pushed the falsehood that Yellowstone water was unhealthy to drink, passengers often bought water for the day's adventure from them at 50 cents a bottle. When the day's tour ended at the Old Faithful Inn, called the largest log cabin in the world, Martha and the "girls" were able to view Old Faithful geyser with the help of a rooftop searchlight installed in 1904. Geyser watching was the principal sport for the hotel guests.

The rest of the tour included Corkscrew Hill, which tested the brakes of their stagecoach (and was often the site of holdups). They may have crossed Yellowstone Lake on a steamship or gone around part of its nineteen-mile shoreline by coach. In either case, they ended up at the Lake Hotel, situated right on the lake, where they experienced a unique serenity. This stop allowed Martha's group to recuperate from their ambitious travels.

On the fifth day the group went down the Yellowstone River past Mud Volcano, past the meadows of Hayden Valley, to the Grand Canyon of the Yellowstone River. Many chose to ride horseback along an eight mile trail (Haines 1977, 121–131). Whether Martha and her girls were bold enough to venture onto the horses is unknown, but the whole tour was full of discovery. Martha noticed that she enjoyed herself around Robert MacBain, who was sensitive and respectful, and full of fun-loving stories. He treated her like an important lady; he made her feel special; and no doubt he made her blush.

As the trip started to wind down, Martha, ever the conscious planner, realized she did not want her joy to end. Though she could not take the enchantment of Yellowstone with her, she might lure Robert to be her needed right hand, and perhaps something else. We do not know if Robert had told her how desperately he was looking for an alternative to farming and teaching, but he saw possibilities in his friendship with this businesswoman. She was kind, sweet, and clearly successful.

Nor do we know if Robert shared how distant he felt from his family because of his inclination to books, his relatively small stature, and his dislike of farming. We do know that he felt shunned by his family and inadequate. He wrote to his trusted sister Grace:

> You may be surprised when I tell you . . . that I always felt I was very much of a misfit. . . . I had to take all the offcast clothes of my older brothers. . . . Did you know I never owned a suit of clothes of my own until I was over 21 years old? . . . the older boys and Bessie got all the

attention and the special breaks. . . . Yes, indeed, I was very jealous and deeply hurt by such a program. All the family used to wonder why I hardly ever went to the community parties and other gatherings—there were two answers—one was that someone had to stay home with mother and by common consent that became me—and two, . . . I never had fit clothes to wear to such places. . . . All the[se] years I've wanted to earn, on my own account, an accepted and respected place within my own family circle. (R. MacBain 1953, 3–4)

In 1912, Robert was ready for a change, but not quite a commitment or even a relationship with Martha. He had had his years of taking care of his mother. But Martha, a determined and patient person, enjoyed this intelligent, charming companion. An eight-year courtship began that gave Robert time, and perhaps the money, to find his way to Rochester, the Harper Method, and ultimately Martha. There was much to overcome: his family ties and their age differences, although at the time it was not uncommon for younger men to marry older women. While he respected, or rather feared, his parents, he felt compelled to separate from them. Their lack of empathy and support had deeply scarred him, and ultimately brought Martha and him together.

Robert's parents had been toughened by the hard choices life dealt them. In the Scottish community of Aberdeen, Robert MacBain, Robert's father, was born in 1834 and became a ship's carpenter. From the church records there, we know that on February 8, 1866, at the age of thirty-one, in Dr. Spence's Presbyterian Church, Robert married Elspet Grassie, a domestic servant, then twenty-four. Their first son, Robert, died in infancy; the two daughters who followed, Robena and Isabella, thrived. But all was not well. As wooden ships began to be replaced by iron hulls, Robert MacBain realized his days as a ship's carpenter were limited. Five years after their marriage, the MacBain family headed for America, land of opportunity (R. MacBain n.d., 1–2).

Like so many other immigrants, they sailed out of Liverpool, on the ship *Erine*. The Atlantic crossing took three weeks, time for Robert to nearly get into a fight with an Italian crewman; it was dramatically broken up by Elspet, who literally put her body between them (R. MacBain 1957). Years later, their son Robert shared with his brother Ed and sister-in-law his reaction to his father's behavior: "No matter who was right or who was wrong in this altercation, I think of it with a sense of pride because it surely reveals that our Dad was a man of spunk and determination and never did nor never would back away from anything he considered his duty or obligation" (R. MacBain 1957). Robert took to heart the need to remain loyal and strong, values Martha would depend on as she aged.

His emotional scars, including his parents' inability to feel for others or each other, brought Martha and Robert together. Painfully Robert recalled how his mother, eight months pregnant, had hiked half a mile with her husband to help him build a barn for a neighbor. Upon their arrival, he realized he had forgotten his tools, and sent his pregnant wife back to retrieve them. Elspet told Robert it was only with God's support that she found the strength to persevere and return with the needed tools (R. MacBain n.d., 3).

Yet, Elspet had her own need to control and had outbursts of cruelty. She hated cats. After neighborhood felines sufficiently annoyed her, she would shoo them into her kitchen, lock the room's doors and windows, and then bang her pot covers together as loudly as she could. The cats went crazy, but Elspet persisted until she was convinced they understood who was master. Then she would open the door, and out they would scamper, as quickly as they could. Elspet just smiled (J. and R. Hoskinson 1996).

These were Robert Arthur MacBain's parents: tough as nails, with little compassion, especially for an odd child. Of their nine children, only their eldest son had died. Robert Arthur, the youngest son, was named after his father and his dead brother; yet, he was always referred to as Arthur within the family, as if he never quite measured up to being a Robert. His three older brothers, Sam, Urban, and Edwin, were all strapping youngsters, much taller than he and more accepting of their destiny to be linked to the land.

Martha also had a cruel father and had felt alone, traumatized, and isolated as a child. She identified with Robert's experiences, and she knew she could change his prospects. It took four years for Martha to convince Robert to join the Harper Method. After that Yellowstone summer, she returned to work. He studied law at Columbia University in New York City under Harlan F. Stone. (Simpson College 1954, 1). Perhaps not so coincidentally, Martha often visited the Harper Shop in New York and others in Connecticut, Maryland, and New Jersey. Besides seeing Robert, there was serious business to take care of. She arranged for an exchange of offices between Harperites and more shops on the East Coast: New Bedford in 1912 and Providence in 1913.

Finally, in 1916, Robert MacBain came to Rochester, New York, as Martha's executive assistant. Over the four preceding years, new developments had unfolded in the industry. The definition of beauty had been shifted from birth-determined bone structure or physical features to beauty aids. This idea democratized beauty; it could be achieved by all women if they used the correct products and treatments.

The link between beauty and popular image became clear, and influenced the emerging beauty industry. Popular stars set the style of what was considered fashionable. To illustrate the connection, Max Factor, the Hollywood makeup artist, launched his own cosmetics business.

During this time, two of Martha's major competitors gained prominence and altered their business strategies. Astutely recognizing that future profits were in cosmetics, Elizabeth Arden introduced them under the banner of facial treatments. Determined to offer the best service, in 1914 she had crossed the Atlantic, in spite of the war's onset, to investigate the finest facial methods used in the top Parisian salons. She visited them all, except for Helena Rubinstein's (her lifelong rival). That same year, in Washington, D.C., Arden opened her second shop. In 1915 recognizing her need for help, Arden married Thomas Lewis, who became a valued business partner but was an unacceptable husband.

In 1917, Rubinstein opened her large-scale manufacturing facility. The next year Arden opened hers. Arden and Rubinstein were converting their salon operations targeted to the elite into what Peiss called "large-scale cosmetics manufacturing, . . . a modern industry. . . . [They each] designed marketing campaigns to reinforce the prestige of their systems, urging women to emulate and vicariously join high society by purchasing costly cosmetics" (*Hope in a Jar* 1998, 87, 88).

Martha continued to open more franchises, supported by her manufacturing arm, but did not target the mainstream cosmetics consumer;

she was in the healthy hair and skin business. In 1917 Robert MacBain received an honorary L.L.B. from McKinley University in Chicago as a result of work done at Columbia. (None of this academic achievement can be verified.) It seems likely that Martha funded his studies. She valued education and probably wanted to share her wealth with Robert; it was like investing in family.

Robert MacBain, at the age of thirty-six, was restless, still searching for a way to prove himself. Responding to his sense of duty and his sense of self, he enlisted in the army; in May 1917, he went to Madison Barracks, New York, to attend Officer Training School. In August, he was commissioned a captain. After training for overseas duty at Camp Hancock, Georgia, he left in May 1918 with the 28th Division (Simpson College 1954, 1). According to *Golden Memories,* Martha waved good-bye to him when he sailed for France (1938, 14).

As an ambulance driver, Robert saw action at Château Thierry, St. Mihiel, and the Argonne up to the armistice on November 11, 1918 (Simpson College 1954, 1). The captain cared about his boys, and they seemed to like him. In his holiday letter to his mother, he described how special they made him feel that Christmas in France:

> [After the entertainment] the 1st Sergeant . . . in a clever little speech presented me with a fine toilet case in leather. It was an elegant thing and must have cost them a lot of money. They also gave me an elegant fountain pen. It made me feel very good to know that the men all felt so generously toward me. They are in reality an unusually fine bunch of men, clean, honorable and gentlemanly. (R. MacBain 1918, 2)

Those men and his military service meant the world to Robert. Using his own skills and contacts, he had performed a man's job well and was respected for his accomplishments. He received five bronze stars and five battle clasps for his performance (Simpson College 1954, 1). When he died, only his military rank and service were recorded on his small, in-ground tombstone. That was *his* performance to be remembered in life and death.

Understandably then, Robert encouraged all to call him "Captain" after the war, as if he wanted to keep alive that moment when he proved himself. He made an exception for Martha who called him Robbie, and he called her Mattie.

Martha was very much a magnet in Robert's life, even during the war. Though no records remain, his niece Esther Meeks stated that Robert and Martha were serious correspondents, making one another feel important and valued. During the war, he sent Martha leather-bound copies of the Bible and Mary Baker Eddy's *Science and Health* (R. MacBain 1945b). These gifts reveal how astutely he understood Martha's religious priorities and how strategically he used his sensitivity to endear himself to her.

A letter Robert sent to his mother about a visit to the Harper Shop in Paris reveals his identification with the organization. We can surmise that Martha may have urged him to visit the Harper Shop in Paris, which he did. In the letter he possessively stated, "Our firm at Rochester has an office there which I had to take half a day off to visit" (R. MacBain 1918, 3).

Notably it was that Paris Harper Shop to which President Woodrow Wilson paid a visit.

> During the negotiations of the Treaty of Versailles, President Wilson found himself under terrible nervous strain. . . . He was so nervously exhausted each evening that he could not sleep. . . . His secretary . . . arrange[d] a private evening appointment for him in the Paris Harper Method Salon, and he was able to enjoy the relaxing massage, brushing and Harper Method scalp preparations. . . . He became so relaxed, completely losing his conference-created-tension that he was able to sleep soundly. . . . So impressed [was] the President, that he had Harper Method equipment installed in the White House. (*Romantic Anecdotes of the Harper Method* n.d., 2)

Robert stayed on in France, according to his Simpson College biography, to pursue more studies, but he kept in touch with Martha. In February 1919, he enrolled at the University of Montpellier, where he took courses in French literature, law, and economics. He published and edited French and English newspapers for U.S. troops attending the school. Upon graduating in July 1919, he received a certificate of merit from the college (Simpson College 1954, 1).

When Robert returned in August 1919, Martha met his ship (Meeks 1996a). His correspondence indicates that he went on to Camp Dix,

New Jersey, where he was discharged, then traveled to Pennsylvania to meet with the families of "his" boys. Eventually he returned to Iowa, and finally, in May 1920, he rejoined the Harper Method, a business he remained associated with until his death.

Thereafter, Robert traveled with Martha as her executive assistant. According to Robert, on a trip to New York City in October 1920, Martha coyly asked him to come to her hotel room, to see her trousseau. Though he readily agreed, he claimed he reacted with some shock, saying, "Martha, I didn't know you were thinking of marriage. Who is the lucky man?" She responded with a wink, "You are" ("Mr. Berry's Comments on Captain MacBain" 1966, 1).

Before they married, however, Martha, had certain priorities a prospective husband needed to accept. She clearly warned him, according to his niece Fausta Ahrens, "Marry me and you marry my family. We come together" (1996). We do not know whether Robert understood that for Martha, her family included her birth relatives, Mrs. Roberts, and her Harper "girls."

Robert agreed, and they promptly married on October 27 in a small Greenwich Village church (Meeks 1996b). At the time Martha was sixty-three, and she discreetly assured that Robert, then thirty-nine, never knew her real age. Her high energy level, youthful spirit, and diminutive height may have masked her actual age; she simply looked matronly. Robert never sought to know her real age.

These were very mature, intelligent people, and they negotiated a deal that made them both happy. They honeymooned in Atlantic City. Robert was decked out in a proper suit and hat, looking like the Beau Brummell he would turn out to be; he proudly escorted his wife, who, dressed in a hat and fitted suit, looked lovingly toward him, beaming with joy (*Golden Memories* 1938, 13). As noted in Banner's *American Beauty*, "For an older woman to have a younger lover became a mark of achievement" (1983, 192). In truth, each was the other's trophy. They had formed a purposeful union.

With marriage to Robert came many benefits: a handsome companion, a trusted friend and business partner, and the automatic right to become an American citizen, which Martha became. Monroe County

Martha and Robert struck a serious pose for their
wedding; he was twenty-four years younger than she.
Courtesy of Golden Memories.

voting records indicate that she cast her first vote in 1923. Martha
registered as a Democrat (like Robert) and thereafter often sponsored
State Democratic Women's Club events in her backyard, where she
entertained governors and other dignitaries (Monroe County Board of
Elections 1923; *Harper Method Progress* Sept. 1933, 10).

There were also liabilities to the marriage. Reportedly, Robert's introduction as Martha's husband was met with consternation by both co-
workers and Mrs. Roberts. An uneasy tension existed between Robert
and John Bushfield, the production manager. Bushfield resented
MacBain's appearance and distinctly called him Mac instead of Captain
(*Harper Method Textbook* 1926, 215).

Martha and Robert on their honeymoon,
strolling along the Boardwalk in Atlantic City.
Courtesy of Golden Memories.

Mrs. Roberts was threatened by anyone who took Martha's attention
away from her, so Robert's presence as a live-in husband was a most
unwelcome, permanent addition to "her" home. Years later, Robert
shared with his niece Esther Meeks that he thought Mrs. Roberts was
impossible. He complained that he had to get her dog chocolates, and
then the "Damn dog wouldn't even eat them!" (Meeks 1996c).

Despite their hostility toward Robert, Bushfield and Mrs. Roberts
retained only warm feelings for Martha. Years later, Mrs. Roberts told
a friend, Mrs. Nellie Wardin "I wouldn't have anything . . . if it [wasn't]
for Mattie" (Re Roberts' Will 1935, 54). John Bushfield was so devoted

MacBain family photograph. On Martha and Robert's first visit to
his family in Iowa, they stood apart (*far right*) from the MacBain clan,
as Robert's relatives looked away from them. Robert's mother, white-haired
and hidden (*center*), was very unhappy. *Courtesy of Fausta Ahrens.*

to Martha that he named his son John Harper Bushfield (Bushfield
1995). Martha's personality and endearing qualities seemed to inspire
heartfelt loyalty among Harperites, but that was not true for Robert.

When it came to the MacBain family, Martha was not well received.
On their first trip to visit them, a revealing family photo was taken. The
photographer caught all heads turning away from Robert and Martha—
that "Scientist," as Elspet MacBain reportedly referred to Martha in a
hissing tone (Ahrens 1997a). The recollections of grandnephew Jack
Hoskinson and nieces Esther MacBain Meeks and Fausta Ahrens indicate that Elspet was most unhappy about the marriage and outspoken
about her son's poor choice. The family consensus was that Robert had
married Martha for her money (Ahrens 1996; J. and R. Hoskinson
1996; Meeks 1996a).

Whatever the reasons they had married, Martha and Robert seemed unaffected by, if not indifferent to, how others viewed them. Each had been a loner, and they now had each other, with all the benefits that brought. Their practical partnership also included genuine affection for one another. Four years after Martha's death in 1950, Robert was awarded an honorary doctorate by Simpson College, his alma mater. Following the ceremonies, he wrote to his sister Grace: "It was a great occasion for me but how I do wish my 'Little Mattie' could have been there too. I did not know she had told you I was smart enough to be President, but it sounds just like a thing she would say. She was so adorable" (R. MacBain 1954).

Martha may have been adorable, but she was also smart. Her marriage to Robert in 1920 coincided with a quantum shift in the process of hairdressing, the lives of women, and the demands made on businesses like hers. In this new era, Martha would direct her business with the help of Robert.

CHAPTER  EIGHT

Roaring Growth

THE 1920S BEGAN FOR MANY AMERICANS as a decade of optimism, complete with "flapper" fashions, bobbed hair, and a carefree lifestyle, all of which spurred dramatic growth in the beauty industry. As Martha Matilda Harper competed in this industry, she retained her distinctive competence, her commitment to good health, her inclusive management style, and her passion to turn working-class women into independent Harper Shop owners and operators. For Martha, it was a glorious time of personal and professional success in spite of (or perhaps because of) her principled approach to the beauty business. Many in the beauty industry promoted significantly different values.

As the internal code of moral restraint was released in the Roaring Twenties, it gave free rein to the commercial exploitation of women's external appearance (Banner 1983, 14, 206–208). This push for outwardly achieved beauty emphasized complexion, which led to the more widespread indulgence in facial cosmetics. While Martha held to her belief that skin stimulation and cleansing led to that "natural healthy look," others advocated externally applied beauty products.

Brilliantly, the industry had convinced women that their beauty was to be found in mass-produced products. This spurred profits because it promoted the concept that beauty could be achieved by all women if they made the correct purchases and obtained the right treatments. Young immigrant women increasingly wanted to look American, as if beauty products would melt their heritages in a caldron and replace those foreign connections with the desired American image. The dean of the American stage, David Belasco, summarized this new reality: "Really all a girl needs nowadays to be a beauty is a pretty body and features not too irregular. Then in steps the beautician, with his or her marcels [stylish waves], and presto!—the plain girl becomes another of the beautiful ones" (Burke Aug. 1930, 12). Elinor Glyn suggested that beauty parlors gave American women "a greater feeling of self-respect and hope amongst all classes" (Banner 1983, 218).

By 1921, American society was aglow with beauty institutions—fashion, cosmetics, and hair culture. Beauty was commercialized and youthful appearance became essential. Lipstick became the most popular beauty product, available in salve, liquid, or stick form. Maurice Levy's 1915 invention of metal containers spurred lipstick's popularity. Rouge and powder gained acceptance, even eye and body makeup (particularly for the legs now visible thanks to the shorter skirts). Nails needed coloring, and the body needed improving through plastic surgery, a skill perfected through the casualties of World War I (De Castelbajac 1995, 56–57).

Other changes were unfolding in society. The middle-class Progressive reformers, who had championed the cause of the poor female wage earner a decade earlier, were now overshadowed by the lure of the "new woman"— the "flapper" who bound her breasts. Meyerowitz summarized the situation thus: "By the 1920s, reformers' earlier image of women adrift, evoking pity rather than excitement, could not compete" (1988, 118). Hollywood, like the beauty industry, used stars to project desirable images reflecting independent, sexually alluring females. The media, with the help of advertising agencies, became powerful allies. Beauty had been redefined.

In response, Martha expanded and repackaged her products to increase market desirability while maintaining her healthful philosophy. In her newsletter, she ran a sample advertisement promoting both the healthful value of her product and its usefulness in hair management. She explained to her followers, "Heretofore we have stressed only the tonic and health value of Harper Tonique and ignored its virtue for keeping waves in and for dressing the hair. . . . Women want anything that makes beauty easier to get" (*Harper Method Progress* July 1924, 6).

Since Martha was both a Christian Science practitioner and a beauty entrepreneur, she maneuvered along a tight balance beam to find her footing in this new beauty market and to preserve her integrity. Predictably, she encouraged advertising in the *Christian Science Monitor* and local newspapers. As the decade unfolded, Harper products were also seen in *Vogue, Ladies Home Journal,* and other women's magazines. In whatever publication, Harper's growing line of products were advertised in a distinctly Harper fashion.

Martha capitalized on the contemporary theme of beauty but gave it a "Harper twist," as this advertisement reveals:

TO BE BEAUTIFUL

Not for a fleeting hour, but always, PERMANENTLY.

The Harper Method and over 450 accredited shops practicing it are showing thousands of women the modern road to beauty through the scientific treatment of the hair, scalp, face and hands. (*Harper Method Progress* Dec. 1925, 121)

During this period, Martha and other female entrepreneurs faced serious competition from a new breed of corporate leadership using different business methods. According to Peiss, these were mostly men who used "a national system of mass production, distribution, marketing and advertising that transformed local patterns of buying and selling and fostered a culture of consumption. By 1920, new cosmetics firms, led primarily by men, embraced these methods to create a mass market and sell beauty products to all women" (1998, 98). To compete, Rubinstein and Arden shifted their strategy to meet the product manufacturing demand. Madam Walker's business, following her death in 1919, was taken over by a man, general manager F. B. Ransom, who used drugstore distribution and media promotion to sell products. He introduced what would become a highly popular product, a skin bleach. This was a product Madam Walker had steadfastly refused to produce while she was alive, and philosophically abhorred (*Peiss* 1998, 113).

In contrast, Martha controlled the direction of her company and the influence of men in her business, and she consistently opposed the

A 1920s Harper trade show. "Miss Ann," Martha's niece, demonstrates the Harper Method. An innovation has been added to the Harper chair—the attached footstool. *Courtesy of Betty Wheeler.*

male-inspired redirection of her industry. However, she apparently ignored the most blatant example of male versus female dominance in this sector. Barbers, mostly male, attempted to prevent hairdressers, mostly female, from cutting women's hair in the new "bob" style. According to the Barbara Burke's *Journal,* barbers dramatically outnumbered hairdressers in the early 1920s (sixty thousand barbers to twelve thousand hairdressers) (April 1923, 17). During these years, the barbers mobilized to pass state laws to assure that only licensed barbers could cut women's hair.

The headlines in the April 1923 issue of the *Journal* warned about the "Barber Menace." The State Board of Barbers presented bills in the New York, California, Illinois, and Oklahoma legislatures to assure that only licensed barbers could cut hair (April 1923, 1). The reader also was updated: "Fight in California, Hairdressers Win" (April 1923, 31). By 1929, twenty-four states had considered barber licensing bills.

The most outrageous outcome of this early twentieth-century sexism was that a woman was actually sentenced to jail for cutting hair. The details were captured in Burke's *Journal:* "For bobbing hair, Madame Florence De Guile, President of the National School of Cosmetology and proprietor of a fashionable beauty parlor, was [given] 30 days in the City workhouse for violation of the State Barber Law. She was charged with cutting hair without a license" (Jan. 1924, 1, 29).

Hairdressers throughout the country fought this spreading barber menace. Sometimes they were successful, as in New York, where both Governor Al Smith and Governor Franklin D. Roosevelt vetoed the bills. Sometimes they failed, as in Wyoming and New Mexico. By 1931, thirty states had laws for barbers, and twenty-two states for hairdressers. A headline in Burke's *Journal* read "Oklahoma Loses Haircutting" (August 1931, 7).

This was a very serious threat to hairdressers, and industry journals alerted their members about the changing legal status of who could cut hair. Yet, not once in this same period did any monthly issue of the *Harper Method Progress* even mention this fight. Why did the problem not exist for Martha Matilda Harper and her Harperites? Perhaps they did not perceive it as their fight, since haircutting to them was secondary to hair and skin care. Perhaps it was simply not Martha's style to confront institutions; historically she chose to invent new approaches rather than win acceptability in an established business system. Perhaps Martha's lack of involvement in the hairdresser battle spoke to her practical focus. Whatever the reason, she and her organization stayed out of this gender-based fight.

Despite (or because of) her noninvolvement, Martha's business boomed and she could not keep up with its demands. Her marriage provided her not only with a charming escort but also with a trusted administrator. Martha increasingly turned to Robert for help with administrative matters. His presence represented a new phase of business management for her organization, allowing Martha to travel, recruit, inspire, locate new shops, and set new directions for the firm. From letters written by

Robert to his mother in October and November 1921, we learn that
Martha and he were often apart while she traveled extensively.

Robert remained in Rochester and concentrated on building their
new headquarters, which would better accommodate the surge in Harper
Shops and the resulting demand for Harper products. The Harper
manufacturing center had been overburdened for years, inefficiently
located both on the Robertses' homestead and in the Powers Building.
The business needed an expanded factory, and Robert ensured that it
was properly designed and built. The new site, at 1233 East Main
Street, was just down the street from the Robertses' home.

Emphasizing the Harper scientific orientation, it was called the "Laboratory," not the headquarters. The brick and concrete structure held a
two-and-a-half-story office operation, featuring a facade with four deco-
rative, cast concrete urns on the roof. "Martha Matilda Harper" was
carved in a rectangular, cast concrete panel located on the cornice above
the central windows, as if the building needed no other identification
(Howk 1996, 2).

Manufacturing took place in the rear section, with "its thousand
gallon glass-lined steel tanks, its steam jacketed vats, its modern assem-
bly of washing, mixing, sterilizing and other equipment" (*Golden Memories* 1938, 15). An elaborate catwalk enabled staff to move across it to
control the opening of various gravity-fed tanks that dripped their distinctive ingredients into mixing containers two stories below. Combus-
tible chemicals were stored in a separate below-ground area.

Although construction had begun that spring, a formal cornerstone
ceremony was held on August 21, 1921, thirty-three years to the day
after Martha's original Harper Hairdressing Parlor opened. Robert
MacBain's memories of that event reveal that Martha initially objected
to being a participant. He nudged her forward, arguing that only she
should select and put the historic items into the cornerstone.

Martha eventually agreed, and placed a number of treasured items
into the cornerstone:

1. Photographs of early Harper associates
2. The first 50-cent piece Martha earned from her business
3. Copies of the Harper patent, product labels, and cartons

The new Harper laboratory and headquarters appeared on a promotional post-card that was widely distributed. On the back of the card, customers were told to "look for the Harper Method Shop in your telephone directory."

4. The Bible and the copy of Mary Baker Eddy's *Science and Health* that Robert had given her. (R. MacBain 1945b)

Martha then explained how her spiritual beliefs influenced her business: "We have laid a foundation today, not of stone, mortar, brick, or any other material substance. We have laid a spiritual foundation upon which, during my whole lifetime, I have tried to build the Harper Method. . . . [It] was founded on Principle and Truth, and . . . it had succeeded . . . only because it had such a foundation" (R. MacBain, 1945b).

By May 1922 the Laboratory was completed, and the building helped meet the surging demand for Harper services and products. It also served as an insular force, encouraging Martha and her network to look to each other for strength. When in the early 1920s, the male industry leaders created and dominated the exclusive National Hairdressing Association (Wynne and Levinger 1995, 4–5), Martha and the Harper network saw no need to join that group, or any group except their own franchise system. Rather, Harperites formed separate regional associations, on the

East and West Coasts as well as in the Midwest. They used national and regional communiqués to keep in touch and share successes and ideas for improvement, and to list opportunities for owners and would-be owners to buy and sell shops.

The *Harper Method Progress*, which was first published in 1923 to provide support to the shops, became an important communications vehicle for Martha's women. Building on her perception of her business as a family, Martha designed the newsletter to share news and achievement, both personal and business. She wanted to encourage an esprit de corps and eliminate discontent. In the Harper newsletter, Martha urged her Harperites to share concerns with her so that all might "co-operate to make our organization 100% mutually helpful and helpfully happy" (*Harper Method Progress* July 1924, 3).

At this time, another publication appeared that advocated for the industry's interests. *Barbara Burke's Beauty Journal* became the official organ of the American Master Hairdressers Association, a group formed for the protection of the hairdressing profession. Barbara Burke, the editor of the breakaway magazine, tried to raise the issue of female leadership in the industry. She believed inadequate attention was given to the hairdressers' cause, and suggested women should take leadership roles.

Burke impertinently asked, "Why Not a Woman for National President?" (Aug. 1923, 17). The next issue of her *Journal* reported that a man had been elected. In 1924, Burke raised the same issue; predictably, again no woman was elected. In 1924 all members of the executive board of the National Permanent Wavers Association were men except for the historian, Madame Louise Berthelon (Burke Dec. 1924, 23). Thereafter, Burke retreated, and her magazine noticeably ceased calling for female leadership.

Perhaps it was because the Harper Method clearly represented female leadership that it found itself essentially blackballed by the industry. Or perhaps it was a matter of financial self-interest; Martha opposed many of their most profitable services. The beauty industry was also being revolutionized by technical innovations in hair dryers, permanents, and marcel curling irons, only some of which were allowed into the Harper shops.

Permanents, banned by Martha because she considered them un-healthy, were aggressively promoted by the industry. Because of declin-ing shop profits and rising competition, permanents were considered the salvation to bring in needed revenue. *Barbara Burke's Beauty Journal* reported that in 1920, 50,000 permanent waves were given; two years later 200,000 American women were having permanents, or 2 percent of all women (Feb. 1923, 26). By 1927, the number of beauty parlors had increased fivefold; thirty thousand beauty parlors then operated in the United States and charged a minimum of $15 per permanent (Burke June 1932, 9).

Martha also opposed hair dyes, and explained why in the *Progress*. She bluntly declared, "Any method of bleaching hair is injurious both to the hair and the general scalp health" (July–Aug. 1927, 86). Yet Martha found no contradiction in her personal use of organic henna to keep her hair remarkably dark even into her eighties and nineties. She often straddled a line of what seemed like two opposites, yet she always made a critical distinction. As she had with being both a Christian Scientist and a beauty magnate, Martha again demonstrated her deftness in defining and adhering to principles. To Martha, organic hair dyes were healthy, and therefore fine to use.

This distinction allowed Martha to proudly announce in her article "Harper Method Wins Again" that hair dyes and skin bleaches were found harmful by the American Medical Association. "Isn't it refreshing . . . that you do not use any of these dangerous substances in your work, and nothing of this nature is manufactured in our Labora-tories. Good old Harper Method! Conservative, perhaps, but absolutely dependable and reliable. Aren't you glad you belong to it?" (*Harper Method Progress* Sept.–Oct. 1927, 124).

However, hair dyes were an increasingly important revenue source for the industry. In 1925 nearly $8 million was collected for those treatments (Burke April 1925, 45). Hair dyes were money makers and were widely promoted. In a later issue of Burke's *Journal*, Julius of Julius Schools had a major column titled, "Boost Hair-Dyeing" that explained why: "Hair dyeing is one of the most remunerative branches of the profession. . . . It does not require considerable salesmanship to convince a patron that she

ought to have her hair 'touched-up' particularly if she is a young woman"
(Jan. 1931, 19).

A look through various issues of the *Journal* leaves no doubt about the
importance of hair dyeing. Advertisements appeared that declared "You
Can Gain Big Profits in Hair Dyeing" (Mar. 1931, 27). In that same
issue, a spokesman for the Ruth Maurer Schools pronounced: "There is
only one thing to think about [hair dyeing]. It's one of the most profitable
branches of beauty culture and . . . the best thing is that the finished job
is only the beginning. Then she has to keep it up" (Mar. 1931, 31).

Under Martha's firm leadership, the Harper Method bucked the trends
and opposed the two most profitable products the hair industry had; she
was viewed by the industry as a rebel. Whether Harper's opposition to
permanents and hair dyes was the reason, or whether her staunch advocacy for female leadership was the threat, Barbara Burke, the communications agent of the national association, was sent to Rochester on
November 19, 1923, to establish the Rochester Hairdressers Association. A review of many issues of *Barbara Burke's Beauty Journal* indicates that Burke rarely traveled to smaller cities. There is no evidence to
prove that she chose Rochester because Harper's headquarters was there,
but it certainly is curious that she did not choose the larger city of
Buffalo and/or the community of Syracuse. Burke selected Mary Lewis
of Dorothy's Vanity Shop to lead the group. Given the options available
to the Association, it does seem that it tried to undercut the pesky
Harper organization.

The Harper organization remained self-sufficient. No Harper staff
member or owner joined the Rochester association, and no mention of
its existence is found in any issue of the *Harper Method Progress*. No
written record explains why Martha chose to be such a loner. Perhaps
she was just too busy, consumed by the demands of her expanding
business. Perhaps Martha simply believed she could take care of her
"girls." Perhaps she believed what she preached: that she had no competitors, as evidenced by her longevity in the industry. Martha had been
operating her business for over thirty-five years when Burke declared in
her *Journal* that beauty culture was "only in its first toddling steps of

infancy" (Feb. 1923, 9). By then, the Harper Method was a mature organization with over three hundred shops worldwide and a clearly enunciated approach quite different from the others.

While proselytizing a different set of core values, Martha was simultaneously fighting a weakening trend in female consciousness. During this period when she was trying to build a pride among her working-class constituency, suggests Estelle Freedman, a historian studying the era, the opposite was occurring in the general society, especially among middle-class women: "The self-consciously female community began to disintegrate in the 1920s just as 'new women' were attempting to assimilate into male-dominated institutions. At work, in social life, and in politics . . . middle class women hoped to become equals by adopting men's values and integrating into their institutions" (1995, 73–74).

Martha did have a female constituency, and she was determined that they recognize their accomplishments. In her June–July 1926 newsletter, she reminded her Harperites about the great achievement of the Harper business. First she stated that the business was complimented by a prominent businessman (perhaps George Eastman?) for the growth of the network from a single shop to a worldwide enterprise. She recalled for her "girls" what their lives had been like before joining the Harper organization: "Some of us . . . [were] . . . broken in spirit; crushed by bereavement; sinking under responsibilities; struggling against the killing routine of monotonous work" (*Harper Method Progress* June–July 1926, 58).

Of course, Martha then identified the Harper Method as their salvation: "The Harper Method has [helped] each of us to become more and more the woman we want to be" (*Harper Method Progress* June–July 1926, 58).

Martha also noted the tangible results of her "girls'" work, enumerating "a growing bank account—a trip to Alaska—the longed-for music-lessons—a tour through Europe—a radio—a string of pink pearls—all sorts of cherished luxuries attained, and ambitions realized for ourselves and our loved ones, because of the Harper Method" (*Harper Method Progress* June–July 1926, 58). Then Martha defined their success:

Successful Harperites, empowered women, delighting in each other's
company. *Left to right:* Mrs. Johnson and Mrs. Cherry from Elmira, New York,
Ida Gorsell from Westwood, New Jersey (fourth figure unidentified), and
Clara Davis from Elizabeth, New Jersey. *Courtesy of Betty Wheeler.*

I believe that the great Achievement of the Harper Method does not
consist of the large number of our shops—though the sun never sets on
them. It is not counted by the daily dollars our cash registers record. It
does not rest on the scientific perfection of our treatments and our for-
mulae, or wholly in the service we give. The Great Achievement of the
Harper Method is the women it has made. (*Harper Method Progress* June–
July 1926, 58)

Unlike other middle-class leaders of the day, Martha knew it was
vitally important that her "girls" acknowledge their hard-earned success.
It was not luck, good fortune, or happenstance; their stick-to-it-ness,
combined with Martha's vision, products, and leadership, was responsible for their financial rewards. While others might be surprised, because they were women—working-class women, at that—their business

success was real. With a charisma equal to any magnetic leader, Martha enlarged her organization by converting ordinary women into proud businesswomen.

Martha's business was an early example of charismatic capitalism as described by Nicole Woolsey Biggart in her book of the same title. Martha and her franchise ownership system enabled her "ordinary" women to transform themselves and to become stakeholders in carrying on the Harper mission. Nearly fifty years later, several direct-selling businesses (Amway, Mary Kay Cosmetics, Shaklee) would follow that model, too, generating billions of dollars for their members and for themselves.

Membership in the Harper system, Martha preached, would yield her "girls" material benefits, just as Mary Kay's workers later could earn pink Cadillacs. It was no accident that in the Harper newsletters, Martha raved about her garden and bubbled about her vacations. Her concluding message was "Just stick to the Harper Method and good old fashioned Principles and you'll wear diamonds of your own make. Then you can go to Europe or do anything else you want" (*Harper Method Progress* July–Aug. 1930, 1).

Martha did not shy away from exposing her own affluence. She saw no contradiction that her franchise system was designed to share profits with her franchisees and that her lifestyle improved greatly as well. Dorothy Riker, a Harper trainee in the 1920s, remembered Martha as "so down-to-earth, you would never know she was a rich woman" (Riker 1995). She recalled that Martha rode the trolley. This was a woman her Harperites could relate to; she was one of them, yet she had money.

Martha and Robert openly shared their wealth, displaying its material benefits with joy. Visiting MacBain relatives effervesced about their experiences in Rochester. Martha and Robert had moved with Mrs. Roberts to a mansion at 853 Culver Road in May 1925 after Mrs. Roberts' home was sold for a sizable sum. The new home had an entire floor they called a dormitory, where Martha's special "girls" stayed.

Visitors recalled how, during the 1920s and 1930s, the house was full of hired help, including a chauffeur, cook, and housekeeper. Guests were elegantly waited on and offered food from silver-covered serving dishes, and finger bowls were placed at each guest's place. Tea might be served from one of five silver sets, or food eaten from one of several sets of good china. Fourteen guests could easily be seated around the dining room table. Robert's niece Fausta Ahrens remembered that a maid brought a glass of wine or sherry to her bedroom every night (1996).

Success, by any standard, had come. By 1931, Martha and Robert were included in Rochester's *Blue Book*, the Who's Who of Rochester society. They were members of the Oakhill Country Club, which enabled Martha to play golf. She had first played at St. Andrews in Scotland while establishing Mrs. Helen Feely's shop in Edinburgh. As the wife of Robert MacBain, Martha was delighted that she could now join this exclusive country club. Predictably, she did not launch a campaign to enable unmarried women to join; her goal was to golf, not to change the country club's rules.

Within the Harper organization, however, female leadership was essential to Martha. Although the newsletter reprinted an ad showing how men were recruited as customers for a Vancouver Harper Shop's men's department, the article made it very clear that though the department was run by a Mr. Glendinning, he was "under Mrs. Glendinning's supervision" (*Harper Method Progress* June–July 1926, 7). The point was made; the husband worked for the wife, reaffirming that the Harper Method was a woman-controlled organization.

With the female issue affirmed, Martha focused her energies on creatively expanding her business and developing innovative ways to attract targeted customer segments. Children were a market she cultivated by establishing children's play areas in Harper Shops. In the *Harper Method Textbook,* she told shop owners how to specifically cater to children: "The child in your Shop should be treated as an intelligent individual. . . . Have a corner in your Shop for this important small clientele, fitted with a little chair and table and a plaything or two. . . . Small patrons of the present make the most loyal and persistent patrons of the future" (1926, 127–28).

Martha even shared her ideas about how to enlarge a beauty business in a November 1929 guest column in Burke's magazine: "Get out after the young folks. Watch your society notes. Be sure to get some kind of letter out to the buds and debs. They aren't so experienced and bored with the advertising as their elders. They are flattered to have arrived with the dignity of being considered a business prospect. Circularize your young married women. Address young mothers. They will find it hard to visit your shop" (Burke Nov. 1929, 46).

Ahead of her time, Martha advocated direct mail, sensitivity to youth, and creative customer recruitment. She shared her insights with the industry, unconcerned that others would copy her ways. As if throwing down the gauntlet, in that same article she bluntly told operators that by producing quality work, they would face no competitors. That was the Harper way.

Similarly, the distinctive competency of the Harper Method was per-petuated because of the strength of its training program. By 1921, the school, no longer an adjunct to the Harper Shop, became a separate facility. In 1922 Martha appointed her trusted niece Ann Harper as the Superintendent of the Harper Training School. "Miss Ann" oversaw the Harper training operations for three decades. Based on its nineteenth-century start, Harper claimed to be "America's First School of Beauty Culture" (*Catalogue of Harper Method Training Schools* 1938, cover).

In 1918, the Wilfred Academy, a school for beauticians, was opened in New York City by two German immigrants, William Zentler and Frederick Korf. The Wilfred Academy also claimed to be America's first beauty school. There is no doubt that Harper's training program oper-ated long before Wilfred ever opened. Martha had trained the staff who operated her 100-plus shops. However, the Harper School as a physi-cally distinct structure opened after the Wilfred Academy.

The Harper Method's training program uniquely provided a differen-tiating guarantee of a lifetime of employability and job placement through its worldwide network of shops. The Harper system integrated recruit-ment, training, and job placement. It offered a soup-to-nuts system of indoctrination, skill-building, and ownership.

A comparison of the *Harper Method Textbook* with the industry's primary textbook, Frederick Korf's *Art and Fundamentals of Hairdress-ing*, published by the Wilfred Academy in 1923, underscores the two organizations' different priorities. Chapter 1 of the Harper text began with the customer, her needs, and the means to satisfy them. The rest of the book elaborated on these themes by reviewing anatomy and the specific methods for giving facials, hair treatments, and shampoos. Customer service and satisfaction were significant topics. Trainees were reminded of the importance of treating children as customers, and the book also discussed the proper treatment of staff.

Korf's *Art and the Fundamentals of Hairdressing* addressed hairdressing as an art, fundamentals of hairdressing and specific types of hair design, and teaching the techniques of hair display. Nowhere were the customer's needs discussed. Korf's textbook promoted the importance of styling women's hair, a surface service, while the Harper book reflected the need for the student's proper understanding of physiology before technique was discussed.

A review of a later textbook written by Christine Moore Howell for black beauticians, *Beauty Culture and Care of the Hair*, suggests that Harper's influence had reached black beauticians. Howell's textbook, like Martha's, concentrated on the scientific aspects of the skin, the hair, and the scalp and on procedures. Howell sounded like a new Harper protégée when she wrote that this was the age of specialization, a time for perfection of the specialist (1936, ix).

These textbooks illustrate that there were very different approaches to training and service; each offered different deliverables. Martha was less concerned with how the customer looked, and much more concerned with how she felt and her overall well-being. Howell seemed similarly concerned about her black sisters. Given this distinction, training was a vital component for Harperites to operate effectively. That is why Martha invested so much effort and staff in this function. With her niece Ann directing Harper training, Martha focused on expanding the rest of the business.

A letter from one of Robert's unmarried nieces, Lillian Hoskinson, to her brother Allen reveals that the original Harper strategy of market segmentation was still used:

> Business is good. . . . Every week brings us one or two of the swells. Just let us have them once and they stay with us.

One of Milwaukee's richest was in Monday. . . . She is very nice and is going to come every week. . . . We also have three cafeteria waitresses and we are trying our best to get rid of them but they seem to stick. We try to keep them hidden when they come in, but oh! They talk so loud and use the worst grammar. . . . Time to work. (L. Hoskinson July 1923)

Targeting of the upper class remained a purposeful Harper strategy. In the *Harper Method Progress*, Martha's column urged owners to uplift their shops, to turn them into classy places. "If your shop has an aristocratic air, your customers will unconsciously like to have it known that they frequent it" (July 1924, 3).

At a time when the industry was pushing mass appeal, Martha continued to focus on marketing to the affluent. American interest in the Harper Method was attributed in the Harper newsletter to European endorsement: "Since the Harper Method abroad is patronized by the nobility, and has written endorsements even from royalty, it isn't strange that the wives of America's prominent men should prefer the Harper Method for their own beautification" (*Harper Method Progress* Sept.–Oct. 1927, 112).

In fact, international government and society leaders used an informal referral network to continue to introduce new clients to the Harper Method. Grace Coolidge, who developed an interest in the deaf after teaching for three years at the Clarke Institute for the Deaf, was taken by her good friend Mrs. Bell to a Harper Shop. Both President and Mrs. Coolidge were very concerned about their hair, and they soon became Harper devotees. During 1923, his first year in office, President Coolidge had Harper hair treatments.

Mrs. Coolidge wore her hair stiffly, in a distinctive horseshoe marcel rolled up around her face, framing her broad features. Ishbel Ross's biography, *Grace Coolidge and Her Era*, stated that while Mrs. Coolidge went to several beauty shops in the D.C. area, "[she] was particularly enthusiastic about the Harper Method" (Ross 1962, 149). Her enthusiasm was so great that when Martha Matilda Harper came to Washington, D.C., Mrs. Coolidge filled her hotel room with an abundance of flowers, including a dozen roses (*Romantic Anecdotes of the Harper Method* n.d., 1).

On a visit to Washington, D.C., Martha's hotel room was filled with
bouquets of flowers, a thank-you gift from First Lady Grace Coolidge,
a grateful Harper customer. *Courtesy of Martha Sweeney.*

Martha's customer base included more than political and social leaders. It included health-conscious people, Christian Scientists, women's
rights advocates, and, in fact, more ordinary businesswomen. The fact
that the Harper Method grew and profited is a noteworthy example of
successful niche marketing. In 1920, when she married Robert, there
were 175 shops; within a year that number had doubled. The Harper
Method network grew each year until the Depression, when there were
over five hundred Harper salons.

While Martha delighted in her business growth and the new management team, on a personal level trouble was brewing. In the early 1920s,
Mrs. Roberts showed signs of diminished mental competence, and became easily swayed by others. Where once Martha was her sole adviser,
now Mrs. Roberts hired a lawyer, Mr. Whitney, and several lengthy legal

For forty-two years, Martha (*left*) took
care of Luella Roberts (*right*).
Courtesy of Golden Memories.

battles ensued. In order for Mrs. Roberts' house to be sold, Martha had
to remove a lien she had placed on it. In exchange, Mrs. Roberts had
to sign releases to Martha's 1894 and 1908 contracts pledging to share
profits with her. The unpleasantness of this exchange did not change
how Martha responded to an ailing Whitney. Her attorney, Frank Dinse,
recalled that she said to Whitney, whom she viewed as a troublemaker,
"You seem to have a bad cold . . . I will send you a few good thoughts"
(F. Dinse 1933, 1702).

Kind as Martha was, she also was a very shrewd businesswoman who
understood the pressures of the times. Some of her "girls" were straying
from her control. With the pressure to be hip and to withstand the
competition from the many other budding beauty shops, some of her

newer shop owners questioned the value of Harper loyalty. Martha understood the power of her personality, and used her columns and speeches to inspire, motivate, and control them. She knew that her leadership provided the glue that kept the network together.

She had to keep her shops and girls in line, even if they were relatives. Grandniece Catherine O'Leary recalled that when Helen Ford, Martha's niece, started operating a shop in Lindsay, Ontario, and erroneously claimed to be a Harper Shop, Martha traveled up to Canada to set things straight. Her niece quickly enrolled in a Harper training program, and her salon ultimately became an authorized Harper Shop (O'Leary 1996b).

At the age of seventy, Martha traveled to the West alone, to visit her shops; wined and dined their owners; cajoled, supported, and trained them. She also closed down imposter operations and tried to quell the concerns over the growing number of competing beauty salons. To maximize the effect, she reported her findings in the Harper newsletter.

> In Rochester . . . we have learned not to become alarmed because of the repeated springing up of beauty parlors. We welcome them. . . . More customers are being made, and if we do the quality work . . . we ought to do, we will get our increased percentage of this same trade. . . . If my Girls would only realize more and more how high grade Harper Method work is compared with the work done in the general run of beauty establishments they would smile instead of frown when they see beauty shops multiplying. (*Harper Method Progress* July–Aug. 1927, 85)

In that same issue, Martha acknowledged that some people suggested the Harper Method had become dowdy and old-fashioned when measured against the changing industry ideal and lucrative procedures. However, she countered that "[Such statements] have been made to me ever since I started my business. I have seen . . . [a woman] leave the Harper Method . . . only to return a much chastened customer later" (*Harper Method Progress* July–Aug. 1927, 85).

Her pitch worked. The Harper Method network rallied and united, for the moment. An outgrowth was the expansion of regional meetings and the formation in some cities, such as Detroit, of a local Harper

Harperites gathered with Martha (*seated at the head of the table*)
on April 27, 1927, at the St. Francis Hotel in San Francisco. The man is
unidentified. *Courtesy of* Catalogue of the Harper Method Training Schools.

association. It became evident that Harper women needed ongoing
contact and support.

The fortieth anniversary of the business was a perfect occasion for an
international gathering at the Laboratory and Martha's home. By Monday,
August 20, 1928, over 253 delegates had registered. A huge tent was
erected in Martha's backyard with bountiful food and entertainment. This
was a time for Harperites to enjoy themselves, experience a change of pace,
and refresh their perspectives by sharing ideas and encouragement with
former classmates or co-owners. Many reported fascination with "a contriv-
ance that looked like a rustic bird-house. On closer examination it proved
to be a telephone, installed so that the house might keep in touch with the
gardener" (*Harper Method Progress* Sept. 1928, 10). They apparently were
delighted that their Martha needed constant contact with the world.

The conventioneers were welcomed by the Vice Mayor of the city,
Isaac Adler; according to reports, his family was one of the early patrons

The Harper Method's fortieth anniversary was celebrated in August 1928. These snapshots are from the lawn party held in Martha's backyard. Martha is being hoisted by her Harperites (*upper left of collage*). *Courtesy of* Harper Method Progress.

of Martha's business. Dr. Walter H. Eddy, Director of the Bureau of Foods and Sanitation of the Good Housekeeping Institute and Professor of Biological Chemistry at Columbia University, was the evening's keynote speaker. He stated that "the Harper Method is scientific because, like medicine, it is based on a study of cause and effect" (*Harper Method Progress* Sept. 1928, 18–19). He also said, "Science (e)ndorses the principles on which the Harper Method is based" (*Harper Method Progress* Sept. 1928, 26).

Then Miss Harper followed. "As she so often does in her talks with Harperites, [she] brought home the importance of right thinking. Without it there can be no right living or right doing" (*Harper Method Progress* Sept. 1928, 19).

Martha Matilda Harper, acknowledged as the Harper guiding light, was presented with a bronze plaque of her image at the opening session. Bronze miniatures of the plaque, with a commemorative notation of the fortieth anniversary of the Harper Method, were given at the convention banquet to each attendee. "And then—the great secret, the diamond brooch given by more than 500 Harperites to the woman to whom they owe[d] so much. . . . Miss Harper was really surprised. . . . 'I had expected to wear rhinestones all my life,' said Miss Harper, 'but now I can wear real diamonds, thanks to my girls. I appreciate this gift more than I can possibly say; just as much, in fact, as I appreciate your being here' " (*Harper Method Progress* Sept. 1928, 3).

Her girls had gotten the message, and they knew that the extravagance of the gift was an important sign of their affluence and their love. It was a time for mutual celebration. In 1927, hairdressing represented a $390 million industry, and the Harper Method had five hundred shops worldwide, a second manufacturing center in Niagara Falls, Ontario, and an ongoing need to recruit and train more and more Harperites.

While the universe was rosy for the Harper Method shops, many unaffiliated shops faltered and others were purchased by large corporate interests. According to Burke, one-third of the business was being done by 7 percent of the shops, and the Harper Method owned a major part of the market (July 1925, 35). A number of successful women business owners sold their shops, including Dorothy Gray, Ruth Maurer of Marinello, Edna Albert, and Marie Earle. Fashion writer Catherine Oglesby observed, "Of the many firms once owned and operated by women the great majority have passed over into the hands of larger companies controlled by men who are directors in large holding companies" (quoted in *Peiss* 1998, 107).

In 1928, Helena Rubinstein sold her American business to Lehman Brothers for $8 million in cash. Because of the 1929 crash, Rubinstein in 1930 bought back her business from Lehman Brothers for $2 million. Also in 1928, a New York City bank offered $1.2 million for the Harper business. Martha and Robert turned it down (Clune 1963, 2A). Peiss, citing the demise of Walker's and Malone's operations, suggested that "Organizations that mingled business and philanthropy could not compete with the single-minded pursuit of profit" (1998, 114).

Martha thought otherwise, and reminded her "girls" in the *Harper Method Progress* that "The Harper Method represents a standard of work that is worth patterning after. . . . I want Harperites everywhere to realize that sticking to the Harper Method faithfully, day in and day out, is the wisest thing they can do" (July–Aug. 1927, 92).

CHAPTER  NINE

Changing Times

DURING THE 1930s, the strength of the Harper Method was tested. Competitive positioning, strategic marketing, and leadership succession caused a fundamental shift in the direction of the Harper empire. First, however, the Harper Method, like the country, had to survive the cataclysmic stock market crash of October 1929 and the economic upheaval it caused.

Following the 1929 crash, when estimates suggest stockholders lost more than $40 billion, an economic collapse resulted that destroyed fortunes and jobs. During the Great Depression, available opportunities were mainly held open for men. Women were encouraged to return home as cultural forces, governmental regulations, and business and union policies combined to restrict their employment opportunities. Marriage bars, formal policies that prohibited women from remaining on their jobs once they married, appeared in schools, organizations, and contracts, and forced the departure of many females from their careers.

The removal of women from wage-earning positions at a time of economic desperation had grave consequences. *Fortune* estimated that in 1932 nearly "a fourth of the nation were members of families that had no regular full-time breadwinner" (De Castelbajac 1995, 62). Such realities became a bind for women as they struggled to support themselves and/or help their families. Because they also faced gender-based wage and career disparities, the degree to which they could help financially was further limited.

For the working-class women whom Martha cared about and employed, the opportunities within the hair care field remained an oasis of

127

self-sufficiency, but often had gender-based limitations. According to the 1940 *Occupational Trends in the U.S.*, in 1890 there were 2,902 barbers, hairdressers, or manicurists; by 1930 that number had grown to 113,194, with women making up nine-tenths of the trade (Anderson and Davidson 1940, 563). Nearly all black women and a majority of white women were general operators, not specialists like four-fifths of the men in the field (Anderson and Davidson 1940, 2).

These women competed with each other and with their male colleagues, who were generally higher paid. In a 1930s study of the field, *Employment Conditions in Beauty Shops*, the Women's Bureau of the U.S. Department of Labor found that women's median weekly earnings were $14.25, with a range of potential earnings from $5.75 to $20.75. Men, on the other hand, had median earnings of $22.50, with a much wider range of potential earnings, from $4.25 to $120.50 (1935, 12-13).

To obtain customers and to generate precious cash, price-cutting became the rage. According to Burke's *Journal*, forty thousand beauty shops were competing with each other. As a result, the industry, including Harper Shops, was plagued by shops that seemed to open "overnight" and that undercut the norms for industry prices. Permanent waves were offered for $1.50–$2.50 and facials, for 50 cents (July 1931, 9).

Martha urged her Harperites to resist such temptation. Reminding them of their distinctive competence and value, she encouraged Harper Shops to differentiate themselves from others by continuing to charge upscale prices. Pride, economic payoff, and market segmentation remained Martha's rallying cry even during these traumatic years when unemployment reached astronomic proportions. Her directions were clearly articulated in her newsletter article titled "Let's Talk the Depression Over":

> If other shops want to give waves, treatments and shampoos for 50 cents, is that any reason why you should work for nothing too? . . . the only way they can make a profit is by doing a tremendous volume of work—which means long hours and generally underpaid assistants and inefficient ones, despite their claims of expert service.
>
> HARPER SERVICE COSTS MORE—IS WORTH MORE. (*Harper Method Progress* Mar.–Apr. 1931, 20)

Even during these difficult years, Martha issued a call to protect the Harper operators. In another issue of the newsletter, owners were encouraged to provide "Fair Play for Employees," as Mrs. Leo Myers's St. Louis shop did. Myers gave her staff half a day off a week to enable them to take care of their household chores. The shop, needing staff to work evening hours to service business customers, rotated night shifts to assure these scheduling demands were not too burdensome. For every evening hour worked, the employee earned two hours off during the day (*Harper Method Progress* July–Aug. 1930, 19). The same enlightened owner held monthly dinner meetings with the staff to help everyone feel connected (*Harper Method Progress* Mar.–Apr. 1931, 4).

These articles reveal the tone and values of the Harper organization during the Great Depression. Martha spotlighted these examples of individual female leadership, cooperation, and mutual support to inspire her Harperites to replicate this behavior. Through these stories, the Harper network was encouraged to view itself as a team of competent women who supported rather than competed with each other. Half a century later, Rosabeth Moss Kanter's book *The Change Masters* suggested that team-oriented organizations were superior.

Martha, however, was no Pollyanna. Recognizing the challenge of the cut-rate competitors, she developed innovative counterstrategies. She urged her "girls" to develop creative marketing ideas to retain their customer base. Martha offered suggestions to stimulate business with an eye toward luring customers with specially timed offers that would not substantially lower the overall Harper price scale. Examples included advertising on Monday mornings or offering services at 25 cents less than the normal price. Another of her marketing concepts was to offer permanents at $8 instead of the regular $10 during March and April (*Harper Method Progress* Mar.–Apr. 1931, 20–21).

An industry publication noted the clever marketing techniques used by the Harper Method. *Barbara Burke's Beauty Journal* recognized how Harper Shops attracted businesswomen and commented that "business women have the money to spend for professional services. . . . Are you taking full advantage of those factors? Why not deliberately advertise to business and professional women—arrange your shop hours for her convenience and needs. Many Harper shops already keep open several evenings each week for her convenience" (July 1931, 9).

In its November 1931 issue, *Burke's Beauty Journal* urged shops to arrange their waiting rooms with customer sensitivity and comfort in mind. This was a concept Martha had specifically advocated years prior, and included in the *Harper Method Textbook*.

During this time of crisis, the Harper Shop owners were also inspired by Martha's philosophy of life. As a result of her childhood struggles, Martha developed a determined ability to face down problems, disappointments, and obstacles. Her approach was to deal with reality and go forward, seek out opportunity, and make lemonade from lemons. She told her "girls" about the power of continual improvement:

> I am a strong believer in the Gospel of Discontent, because . . . [b]eing satisfied with things as they are is a sure sign of decline.
>
> . . . Constructive Discontent, is to me, a higher faculty of mind. Through its force, women now occupy, as never before in history, positions of responsibility, usefulness and freedom. . . .
>
> A Wholesome Discontent . . . will bring us better things in the future, will make our lives fuller and more interesting, and will bring us prosperity and success, and crown our lives with joy and happiness (*Harper Method Progress* Mar.–Apr. 1930, 1)

Martha's ability to deal with difficulties and to develop creative solutions guided her Harper empire through the early 1930s. In 1931 she observed with pride how well her network had survived the Depression. Notably, her declaration was based on a businessman's statement affirming the success of her enterprise. She first cited his complimentary statement before she affirmed the value to Harper Shops of their affiliation with the Harper Method:

> I heard a story the other day that made me feel good when everyone is talking about hard times. . . .

All of the men were high-class, [business] men. One of them said, "Well what business can you go into now, if you want to be sure of success and not failing." Another man spoke up and said, "The Harper Method is the only one I know where you can do that." . . .

And isn't it true? . . . Other businesses have failed, but we've not had a single shop close on account of hard times. (*Harper Method Progress* Mar.–Apr. 1931, 1)

Martha Matilda Harper's empire had followed her strategic plan and survived the Great Depression relatively well.

However, Martha's challenges were not yet over. Luella Roberts had died on February 24, 1930. Her death was a major loss for Martha, but her will brought the biggest shock. In 1913, Mrs. Roberts had written a will, which Martha had seen, leaving everything to Martha. Unbeknownst to Martha, that will mysteriously disappeared and was replaced by another, drawn up in 1925 when Mr. Whitney started representing Mrs. Roberts. That second will left the majority of the Roberts' estate to a variety of charitable institutions, established Whitney as the executor, and gave only a small amount to Martha. Intending to squelch objection, it contained language indicating that if the will was contested, the would-be recipient would lose her share[s].

Notwithstanding the clear threat, Martha challenged the document. A six-year legal battle ensued; atypically Martha, who normally found ways to achieve her goals by creating her own path, chose to legally confront her adversary, Mr. Whitney. Although her legal battle occurred while Martha was struggling to maintain her franchise network's profitability and the morale of her franchisees, she followed her positive thinking and action. Ultimately the Appellate Court ruled for Martha and the parties settled (Re Roberts' Will 1935, 55; M. Harper 1933). It was a bitter victory because, once again, a trusted "family" member had let Martha down. It would not be her last disappointment with her family.

The other test Martha and the Harper Method faced was responding effectively to a changing industry that forced major consolidation and encouraged an intensely competitive marketplace. Demand for consumer products grew, and the distribution network focused on wholesale. In 1932, Charles and Martin Revson and Charles Lachman formed Revlon, a nail polish firm that offered more choices of nail polish shades. In 1932, Maybelline brought out its mascara for eyelashes. And in a 1936 issue of *Mademoiselle* the term "made-over" was used, thus formalizing the concept of a makeover. (Peiss 1998, 144). During this decade, more cosmetic indulgences were created and offered. Elizabeth Arden produced an eight-hour cream. Rouge, though still popular, had more subtle shades. Lipstick now came in a rainbow of colors.

In response, the Harper Method edged into more serious product manufacturing and marketing. Martha cleverly revealed her firm's broader distribution system in the winter issue of the *Progress*. Using religious and personal anecdotes, she reminisced in her column how, at the age of seventy-four, she had recently strolled in the woods near where her Canadian family lived. Martha then announced a new Harper distribution approach: "I told my husband the other day that I didn't care what happened to me now, that I could die happy, because I had done something I've always wanted to do. All my life, I've wanted to put Harper Method goods in the department stores and now we're doing it" (*Harper Method Progress* Nov.–Dec. 1931, 1).

Delicately, Martha had pulled off the introduction of Harper products into department stores while keeping her shop owners supportive. She used it as a lesson in pure Harper win-win philosophy. If the base of Harper customers could be enlarged by using department stores, then shop owners would benefit from additional demand for services. Proudly she announced that Harper products were now in Boston at Jordan Marsh stores. Sibley, Lindsay and Curr carried them in Rochester, as did Dey Brothers in Syracuse, Shephard's in Providence, Rhode Island, H. and S. Pogue in Cincinnati, and most of the major department stores throughout the United States. This, the shop owners were told—and they came to accept—was progress. In fact, Martha had led her organization into the mainstream retail distribution channel: department stores.

Martha hired Joanna Hubbard, a staunch Christian Scientist, to become Harper's first traveling representative, what the industry called a

A display of Harper Method products at the Jordan Marsh department store in Boston. Martha's photo hangs on the right and that of the Harper Laboratory on the left, amid the many Harper retail products. *Courtesy of Betty Wheeler.*

demonstrator. This position, new for Harper Method, had been used for years by Rubinstein and Arden, as well as others. Nevertheless, Martha presented the creation of this position as a coup.

An issue of the Harper newsletter explained that Hubbard's job was to travel the New England and Middle Atlantic territory, visiting with shop owners and department store representatives, presenting the latest Harper products, and explaining their benefits. Later, Alice Wright covered the southern states (*Harper Method Progress* July–Aug. 1932, 24–25). Increased outreach and sales were becoming important in order to compete within a media-conscious industry.

Media stories were generated that publicized the Harper Method. Martha had been featured in a *Democrat and Chronicle* series titled "Who's Who in Rochester Business." The story reported that there were five hundred Harper Method branches in "practically every civilized country." Martha was presented as a well-rounded community citizen, businesswoman, and wife who enjoyed entertaining and was a member of the Women's City Club, the Memorial Art Gallery, the Eastern Star, the Rochester Historical Society, and the American Legion Auxiliary (*Harper Method Progress* May–June 1931, 4).

On a national basis, the media were used to inform the public that men used the Harper Method. In an article titled "Baldness," *Fortune* magazine reported that "[the Harper Method] is perhaps the name most widely known in the hair cultivating industry. . . . Stout Christian Scientist, [Miss Harper] . . . makes no claim to cure baldness, but is reasonably sure she can prevent it (1933, 55). Martha's reputation in this area explained why men as well as women enjoyed the Harper Method; in fact, according to Harper Shop owner Centa Sailer, nearly 15 percent of the Harper method clientele was male, serviced in a private section or room. Men with important jobs luxuriated in the scalp massages as they escaped the stresses of their lives.

Prior prestigious customers' names were cleverly mentioned in that issue of *Fortune*, as if to encourage others without revealing the names of current celebrity patrons: "[Miss Harper] . . . has many a famous client, [each] name carefully guarded. Woodrow Wilson was for years a faithful patron. . . . And for the past quarter of a century, all Presidents' wives have been Harper patrons. Mrs. Hoover broke the chain" ("Baldness" 1933, 80).

Such positive press exposure increased the Harper empire's credibility. Yet, despite this public exposure, the Harper world, with its commitment to individual success of women through cooperative business support, held little credibility in the larger world of business. It was not its radical structure, the franchise, that was the problem; it was the gender of its president.

Martha was not the only woman to be ignored as a significant business force. Despite the fact that the beauty industry was reported to be the nation's fourth most significant (*Burke's Journal* May 1932, 7), the successes of Madam Walker, Annie Malone, Helena Rubinstein, Elizabeth Arden, and Martha Matilda Harper were summarily dismissed by the business community because they were women. *Fortune* magazine, having documented the societal restrictions on women workers in factories and offices, concluded in the last article of its 1935 series "Women in Business" that women lacked the ability to lead an industrial, competitive corporation.

Sixteen exceptions prove the rule that woman's place is not the executive's chair. . . . There is no American woman whose business achievement would properly rank with the first or the second or even the third line of male successes. . . . Elizabeth Arden, [Helena Rubinstein], and her kind, in other words are not professional women. They are women by profession. And as such they do not belong in an enumeration of women industrialists. . . . Elizabeth Arden is not a potential Henry Ford. She is Elizabeth Arden. It is a career in itself, but it is not a career in industry. . . . [They are] women engaged not in general business in competition with men but women engaged in the business exploitation of femininity—theirs or another's. ("Women in Business III" 1935, 81)

What is particularly telling about this article is that money, often a measuring stick of success, was no longer used by the magazine as such an index. Instead, *Fortune* acknowledged that these women earned enormous amounts of money: "Elizabeth Arden is reputed to have made $700,000 in 1929. Helena Rubinstein has made as much or more" ("Women in Business III" 1935, 81, 86). In fact, in 1930 Rubinstein had made over $6 million by selling her business, but according to *Fortune* that was not industrial money, nor were the chemists, labs, and factories these women supported real. Years earlier and later, however, *Fortune* had spotlighted and would spotlight the corporate successes of Colgate-Palmolive and Revlon, companies geared toward the soap and beauty businesses, respectively, businesses run by men.

Fortune's article underscores the irreverence with which it viewed businesswomen's accomplishments. Arden and Rubinstein had, in fact, used traditional male business techniques, yet their successes were written off by *Fortune* as unworthy of the corporate business community. The nontraditional approaches employed by Martha Matilda Harper,

Annie Malone, and Madam Walker were not even mentioned, and thus were dismissed all the more easily.

Ironically, it was Martha's female identity that galvanized the customers, the operators, the franchisees, and the overall Harper network. Together they formed a powerful force to change both their own destinies and the complexion of American business. Yet the female leadership so critical to the success of the Harper Method was about to change. This transition represented the most challenging survival test yet for the business.

Notably, Martha Matilda Harper's departure as President was never explicitly announced to her faithful. Instead, Martha's column in the November–December 1932 issue of the newsletter discussed loyalty. It recalled how she had remained loyal to her "girls" during this year of difficulty, and how loyalty was critical to the organization: "The past year . . . I have felt it my duty, as well as my great privilege, to remain strictly and absolutely on the job all the year so that I might hold myself in readiness . . . [for my] pressed girls. . . . Loyalty, to my mind, is one of the most essential virtues. . . . Beware of all such temptations to . . . cut loose and follow an independent course [from the Harper Method]" (*Harper Method Progress* Nov.–Dec. 1932, 1).

Only a careful reading of that newsletter's masthead would have alerted the reader that Martha, seventy-eight years old, was now Founder and Vice President. She had essentially stepped aside, and although she remained a titular personality for the organization, the business was now in her husband's hands. To some it would seem a logical transition; to the Harper organization it was a new paradigm.

Robert had been quietly promoted to President, and John Bushfield, General Manager of the Harper Method, disappeared from the masthead. Bushfield had been the "impertinent" thorn in Robert's side who refused to call him "Captain," as everyone else did. As Bushfield's son (Harp) remembers it, his father was fired by Robert MacBain. Harp recalled in an interview that "My mother blamed Robert MacBain" for his father's subsequent death of a heart attack (Bushfield 1995).

Canadian Harperites gathered at a meeting in 1932 without Martha.
Courtesy of Betty Wheeler.

According to DBA (doing business as) records at the Monroe County Clerk's office, Bushfield set up Bushfield Laboratories in April 1932; however, according to Betty Wheeler, a later Harperite, the Harper talk was that he improperly made products using Harper-based formulas. Bushfield was a chemist, a graduate of Oberlin. The Harper Method sued to prevent him from allegedly manufacturing their products. Today, the contentions of neither side can be verified, but Bushfield definitely set up his own laboratory that operated long after his death.

In 1932, the identity of the Harper Method changed as Robert MacBain took over. With him directing the company, the *Harper Method Progress* became a more obvious marketing tool. The section devoted to customer feedback, "Boosts and Knocks," was eliminated. Instead, the newsletter placed major emphasis on product and service promotion. An advertisement featured in the May 1933 issue reflects a noticeable change in philosophy. The Harper scientific methods were touted as the means to create powerful products capable of visibly changing a person:

TAKE THIS SURE ROAD TO CHARM

Charming people are made, not born. And you'd be surprised how many of them acquire their chic right here. For forty-five years the Harper Method and its scientific preparations have been bringing lustre to neglected hair and the glow of youth to tired skin. Let us show you what a series of inexpensive treatments can do.

THE HARPER METHOD SHOP. (*Harper Method Progress* May 1933, 8)

This advertisement captured the schizophrenic message the Harper Method started to project in Martha's absence. Twisting its scientific reputation, the Harper Method repositioned itself as a "me-too" mass-oriented beauty firm. In 1926, the *Harper Method Textbook* had taught that the Harper operator's role was to release a woman's inner beauty. Now the advertisement reflected a different philosophy. Charm could be manufactured by and purchased from the Harper Method. Just like other beauty salons of the era, the Harper Shops were ready to make customers charming. The distinctive competence of the Harper Method with its healthful skin and scalp treatments and organic-based products remained, but its compelling distinction was blurred by the more trendy promotions.

There were other notable changes in the business. A fundamental shift occurred without Martha to hold the organization true to its principles. In the 1920s Martha had railed against "unsafe" permanents. After she left the business as CEO, permanents were introduced. An ad promoted the Harper Method permanent wave machine as being "a Depression cure, just what the doctor ordered, a way to combat price competition" (*Harper Method Progress* May 1933, 16). Allegedly the Harper machines were safer than the competitors', but it was clear that they were created to meet market demand. In another issue of the *Progress,* various Harper products were displayed with the headline "Profit by the Jar" (*Harper Method Progress* Mar. 1935, 4).

In keeping with this new fashion and profit sensitivity, the *Harper Method Progress* announced in August 1938 the launch of the Harper

Method Hair Crayon, designed for "people with slightly greying hair who wish to make the grey hair less conspicuous. . . . Miss Harper is thrilled about it and Miss Ann uses it on many of her customers" (5). This statement is particularly revealing. By citing Martha's alleged enthusiasm and her niece's use of the product, the newsletter implied that this was an acceptable product in spite of Martha's former disdain for such items. The Harper business was markedly changing, but it could not complete this transition without claiming it had Martha's endorsement.

Yet, the importance to the Harper organization of women's economic independence was not totally lost. An article documented how Ava Butler, a California shop owner, had put her son through college with her shop earnings (*Harper Method Progress* Sept. 1933, 7). The message to Harper franchisees had a familiar ring. Women could reap material benefits by being a Harper Shop owner.

Proud of the Harper tradition and sensitive to its female base, Robert struggled to find the right balance to retain a competitive edge in an increasingly cut throat industry. He modernized Harper's image and advertising appeal, and tried to satisfy a different consumer market, without the creative genius of Martha, who had used changing themes to strengthen the Harper appeal.

Robert's efforts, in fact, eliminated some of the Harper distinctiveness and clearly shifted the firm away from its highly successful use of market segmentation. He only partially succeeded in repositioning the company as a leader in the market. The effect of his efforts was to compromise the proud and powerful Harper market. An early Harperite, Dorothy Riker, remarked, "It was her husband, who commercialized everything too much" (Riker 1995). The core competency to which Martha had so valiantly held her business true, began, slowly, to be compromised as the Harper Method followed fashion and industry pressures.

The Harperites were changing, too. Because of both the growing number of Harper Shops and the departure of the older pioneers, it was increasingly important to recruit and motivate a new cadre of Harperites. These recruits had not been servants, and thus were less loyal, more inclined to follow society's call for women to return home and become homemakers, mothers,

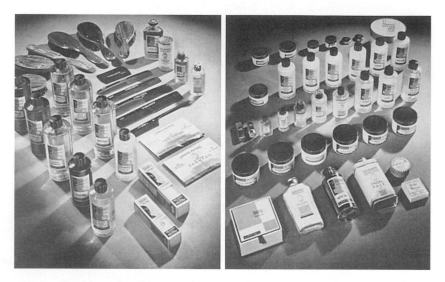

Display of updated packaging for Harper products, 1938.
Courtesy of Golden Memories.

and wives. It would take decades for the redirection to have its full impact, but it began under Robert's stewardship.

No longer was Martha the articulate leader countering the social pressures that encouraged women to "define themselves by their physical appearance" (Banner 1983, 100). No longer was there a strong, principled woman who was their active role model; who encouraged ambition, kindness, and creativity from her franchisees and workers; and who understood how to attract and then delight the dedicated Harper customer base. Those values and qualities remained echoes in the Harper operation, but they no longer were clarions trumpeted by the leadership.

Instead, as the industry moved ahead, salon fever seemed to have overtaken the world. Max Factor opened his salon in 1936 with over eight thousand invited guests. Lancôme in Paris opened one in 1936. Elizabeth Arden expanded her network of salons to twenty-nine even though they were not profit centers (De Castelbajac 1995, 78). Arden's cosmetics subsidized her salons, which combined exercise and yoga, cosmetics, fashion, and specialized treatments. A firm believer in fitness and yoga's benefits, Arden used her salons as temples to proselytize and

The Harper Salon in Santa Barbara, California, run by Mrs. E. Goff.
Courtesy of Betty Wheeler.

also to sell her products. According to Arden in the film *The Beauty Queens,* her system took "total dedication to vanity. . . . Everything is planned for you to be absorbed with yourself" (Hersa 1988).

As competitors fought each other, the government began regulating the industry. The July 1937 issue of *Drug and Cosmetic Industry* suggested that the industry had recognized it was in "the age of science which looks for evidence and fact" (De Castelbajac 1995, 80). In 1938 the Federal Food, Drug, and Cosmetic Act was passed; it subjected cosmetics to the stricter regulations that applied to drugs. Now inspections were required, labels were relevant, and ingredients needed to have governmental approval. These were issues with which the Harper Method had long complied, but other manufacturers had opposed. The core scientific base (and organic products) of the Harper Method served the organization well.

Eunice Galloway Van Alstyne, Harper training
center instructor, in her uniform.
"Miss Ann" took Van Alstyne, an orphan in
need of a career during the Depression, under
her wing. She allowed her to train at the
Rochester school and to pay off her tuition with
earnings from her Harper job. Notice Harper
pin and embroidered HM on her cap.
Courtesy of Eunice Galloway Van Alstyne.

The other important cornerstone of the Harper Method—training—
remained intact. The Harper School provided one of the best training
programs in beauty culture, and competitors quickly hired away Harper
trainees. This encouraged would-be recruits to sign up as trainees. As a
result, Harper training became a more valued money-making business.
By 1938, the Harper Method had training centers located in Rochester,
Madison, Wisconsin, and Winnipeg, Canada. Later the number of schools
grew to five, with the two new ones located in Atlanta, Georgia, and

Vancouver, Canada. Tuition in 1938 was $175 and the hours of study varied, depending on state requirements, though generally the training took about six months (*Catalogue of the Harper Method Training Schools* 1938, 8–9).

In addition, 1938 marked the fiftieth anniversary of the Harper Method. Such a momentous milestone was an occasion for Harperites to rejoice. The September 1938 issue of the *Harper Method Progress* described the weeklong Golden Jubilee Convention. Hundreds of Harper Shop owners and staff streamed into Rochester to celebrate Martha's past leadership and Robert's new role. It had been a decade since they had all gathered. In the interim, they had weathered the Depression and were optimistic about the future.

Early in the week, the Harperites were greeted by Rochester Mayor Lester Rapp and Chamber of Commerce President Warren Parks. Then Captain MacBain honored his wife by describing her strength of character, courage, and tolerance. The Harper history was recounted, and that evening a special ceremony saluted the more than eighty living pioneers, Harper women who had over twenty-five years with the company and still operated Harper Shops. Martha said it was the "most thrilling occasion." The oldest attendee was Miss Kathleen Sullivan, who opened her shop in St. Paul, Minnesota, on April 5, 1897. Bertha Farquhar had died May 2, 1932 (*Harper Method Progress* Sept. 1938, 1, 5, 9).

Tuesday, August 23, was Martha Matilda Harper's day. It began with a "Pageant of Progress," a review of product changes beginning with Martha's little brown jug containing the precious hair tonic and the unique Harper shampoo bowl. Attendees also learned that raw materials for Harper products came from around the world, and were made aware of the great distance some raw materials for Harper products had traveled. The purposeful use of these raw materials underscored the Harper distinctiveness.

The facts about the raw materials were meant to inspire Harperites with pride about their products. According to the September 1938 issue of the *Harper Method Progress,* "musk tonquin" was imported from China to make Harper perfume, as was coconut oil for shampoo. From France, Italy, and Spain came the olive oil used in Harper creams, brilliantines,

At the Golden Jubilee, Martha was seated center stage. She was called the "Queen of the Festival" by her Harperites who came to celebrate the fiftieth anniversary of the Harper Method. Robert MacBain, the new president, stands behind his wife. *Courtesy of* Harper Method Progress.

and salves. An herb from Yugoslavia was required for Harper Tonic. Russia provided the Siberian boar bristle essential for the strong Harper Method brushes, as well as a tonic ingredient. Germany sent chemicals and a high grade of lanolin for Harper creams. A wax used in Harper creams and lotions came from Norway and Sweden. Britain delivered lavender oil and a high grade of almond meal. From Madagascar came the quince seed for finger waving and face lotions. On the list went, including imports from the East Indies and South America (*Harper Method Progress* Sept. 1938, 4, 11).

From the Laboratory, a parade of four hundred conventioneers marched to the MacBain home, where a garden party was readied— food, entertainment, and soaring spirits blended with the picture-perfect day. According to the newsletter, the climax was the presentation of gifts to Martha. In keeping with the Harper consciousness of hard-earned dollars, these gifts were extravagant:

> The shop owners presented her with an arm chair done in gold brocade symbolizing the 50th Anniversary, . . . a beautiful silver tray of large proportion; and to complete this gift again the shop owners came forward to present a [distinctive] silver tea and coffee service—showing the cooperation between operators and shop owners. . . . If all this were not enough, Miss Harper was embowered with flowers. When she sat on the gold chair she looked like a queen on a throne. . . . she was crowned by the youngest Harper to take up the work. (*Harper Method Progress* Sept. 1938, 2)

At the Golden Jubilee, Martha was crowned by the Harperites with fifty
golden rosebuds and given her "golden throne" (*upon which she is
seated*), a golden mesh bag (*on her lap*), and an engraved Art Deco
silver tea service (*seen in lower right on table with the set of Robert Burns's
works given to Robert*). *Courtesy of* Harper Method Progress.

The Harperites presented Robert, their current leader, with a leather-
bound set of the works of Robert Burns; it was a generous and sensitive
choice. As a loyal Scotsman and a man who treasured the written word,
Robert cherished the gift for the rest of his life. However, Martha's gifts
were more extravagant; she was their heroine and it was to her that they
gave their prime loyalty and the greatest proportion of their precious
dollars.

The September newsletter detailed how on Wednesday, the day of
speechmaking, tributes were read. They had poured in from around the
world and were wildly applauded by the more than four hundred Harperites
attending the Hotel Seneca banquet. Governor Lehman and dignitaries
from around the nation sent accolades that were read. Eugene Van Voorhis,

Martha's first attorney, led the speakers' list and described her as the "soul of generosity." He also remembered that she possessed the " 'fighting spirit,' determined that right must predominate." The accolades continued:

> Mrs. Meta Fay [an early customer in Washington, D.C.] . . . personally presented Mrs. Roosevelt's greetings. . . . [She lauded] in very strong terms, Miss Harper's humanitarian spirit and the love she holds for her own sex.

> Mrs. Steinhausen . . . then enumerated Miss Harper's crowning achievements—not the accumulation of wealth—but her modesty; her desire to help humanity; her vision and serene assurance. She related how many women in history have ruled through inheritance and force, but Miss Harper reigns through intelligence, service and sacrifice. (*Harper Method Progress* Sept. 1938, 2)

As the Golden Jubilee demonstrated, Martha was the honored ceremonial leader; however, a new operational team had taken over. At this celebration, Robert MacBain introduced the newly hired merchandising and promotional manager, Earl Freese, a marketer from Bell & Howell of Chicago, All American Radio, and Sheaffer Pen (*Harper Method Progress* Sept. 1938, 2). In addition to Freese, two other experienced marketing men, Warren Wheeler and James McGarvey, became Harper executives. It was a male-led, mass-marketing team.

While the Harper Method was under Martha's firm direction, it proclaimed itself to be an independent, female-conscious organization. Women of little means bonded throughout the world, enriched and empowered by this Harper ideal and the Harper network. When Martha no longer led the organization, that message began to change, ever so slowly and subtly.

Martha's successor and his team seemingly were left alone to redirect the business. Martha yielded control to her husband, just as so many younger women were encouraged to do when they married, usually early in their lives. Martha, who purposely waited until she was sixty-three years old and her business was secure before she married, had been working since she was seven years old. In 1938, now eighty-one years

old, she may have been tired, ready to let go of her commercial responsibility and lead a less stressful life, ready to give up her vigilance and
vision. Or she may have simply been an aging woman whose mental
faculties had begun to fail. Whatever the reason, Robert wanted the
Harper Method to join the economic mainstream of the beauty business, and Martha, tired and/or old, wanted or needed a different lifestyle.
They both got their wishes, but at a cost to the Harper Method that
would not be measured for decades.

CHAPTER TEN

Letting Go

IN THE EARLY 1940S, as the world focused on war, Robert exercised his influence over the Harper organization while Martha, who was in her eighties, increasingly turned inward. The tone of Martha's columns in the monthly newsletter changed noticeably; they focused on her gardens and vacations, and only periodically were visits to Harper Shops mentioned. It was soppy verbiage, not the radical talk about women building the Harper business that she had espoused in the 1920s. Once Martha had been the articulate pioneer who supported a new vision for women and encouraged them to be "positively discontent" with their circumstances. In the 1940s, she was a make-believe force. Her columns were now ghost-written, portraying a very traditional female image.

Martha seemed as oblivious to her image change as she did to how government viewed the beauty business. In 1942, the U.S. War Production Board ruled that cosmetics were not an essential commodity. Within months, after powerful lobbying, the Board rescinded its restrictive production edict with a statement that "cosmetics [were] 'necessary and vital products' contributing to the morale and well-being of women engaged in the war effort" (De Castelbajac 1995, 94). No wonder that in 1943 Tangee ran an ad promoting its lipsticks in the *Ladies Home Journal* with a headline that read "War, Women and Lipstick" (De Castelbajac 1995, 90).

Sales-oriented advertisers were not the only ones who promoted cosmetics. Women increasingly were lured to join the war effort with the expectation that they could, if not should, look good while doing a "man's" job. Beauty salons and charm classes were offered at airplane factories including Lockheed and Boeing. The All American Professional Girls baseball teams, formed during this period, mandated that their players take lessons in makeup from Helena Rubinstein. Even psychiatrists supported the concept that women's attractiveness would increase productivity and morale (Peiss 1998, 241–242).

There were sacrifices to be made for the war. In March 1942, the U.S. government mandated that hair salons gather hair clippings which were then mixed with rayon fibers to make cloth. Cosmetics, though widely promoted, became more scarce and thereby more expensive, and were used sparingly. Yet new sales opportunities opened as the war caused changes in product usage. Because stockings were in short supply, women began to paint their legs with a "stocking shade of body makeup" (De Castelbajac 1995, 91).

Before the war, Martha stayed at home while Robert and his management team reevaluated the direction of the Harper organization. They properly assumed that the core Harper customer base was solid, and continued to encourage such identification. Among the movers and shakers of society, the Harper network remained a nationally recognized institution. The June 1941 issue of the Harper newsletter noted that "a permanent display of Harper Method products and a sketch of the grand accomplishments of Martha Matilda Harper [was] exhibited in [a] Dallas building of the Historical Association of American Women" (*Harper Method Progress* June 1941, 10). The Harper name and legacy remained a valued institution.

Because confidentiality and distinctive service were a hallmark of Harper Shops, the shops continued to attract prominent customers from society and the theater, including Helen Hayes, Eddie Cantor, Danny Kaye, the Marx Brothers, Irene Dunne, and Dinah Shore (Wheeler 1996). To serve them, an early Harper policy was changed; shop owners selectively agreed to service important people at their homes. While Rose, Eunice, Pat, Kathleen, and Jean Kennedy all patronized the Harper Method Shop in the private Everglades Club on Worth Avenue in Palm Beach, Florida, the family patriarch, Joseph P. Kennedy, had Harper operators come to his house. One of those operators, Jane Reed, described the experience:

Weekly, I would arrive early at the Kennedy compound. . . . Mr. Kennedy
was quite cordial and full of jokes while I gave him a scalp treatment
which took nearly 45 minutes or more. I was paid weekly, although I
must confess, Mr. Kennedy was not very generous with the tips.

Those with the real societal panache were our customers too, the DuPonts,
the Vanderbilts, the Donahues, the Graham Bells, the Fords, and Hearst
families. But, the truth was we treated everyone as though they were
important. (Reed 1997)

While this affluent customer base remained intact, Robert hoped to
attract a greater share of the mainstream market. By 1944 a Harper cold
permanent system was developed. This broader outreach was shown in
the summer 1944 Harper newsletter, which previewed an ad that would
run in the September issue of *True Story*. The headline read "Romance
follows a Lovely Skin . . ." and the text emphasized that "loveli-
ness . . . wins romance and admiration." The ad also offered a free chart
detailing the Harper Method treatments for twenty-two different skin
problems (*Harper Method Progress* July 1944, 12).

Both the ad and its placement reflected the change in the Harper
market appeal. The ad was placed in a mass audience publication rather
than the more literary *Christian Science Monitor*. By co-opting the no-
tion of romance, the ad tried to appeal to the masses, yet what was
actually offered was a come-on to pursue the scientific skin treatment
system Martha had perfected. It was the same Harper Method, slightly
repackaged.

To update shop owners and operators on new product offerings and
changes, the Harper Method initiated a free graduate training course.
The issue of retaining loyal Harperites increasingly surfaced as the cadre
of early pioneers continued to die or retire. The change in Harper
staffing even influenced how the integrity of the Harper franchise was
enforced.

In 1940 the newsletter reported that a Standards Committee was
formed to "protect Authorized Harper Method Shops against those
who would infringe or trespass on their rights and privileges" (*Harper
Method Progress* March 1940, 1). Where once such enforcement was

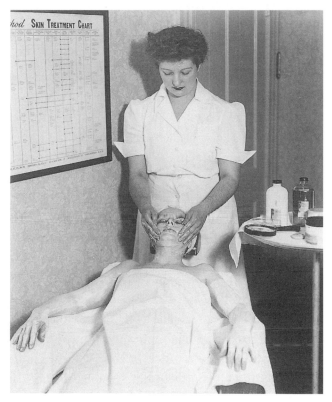

A Harper facial being conducted. The skin treatment
chart is at the left. *Courtesy of Betty Wheeler.*

based on trust and personal oversight, in the 1940s more formal procedures were necessary. Even Martha's column urged owners to alert
the organization to any infringers.

Other challenges persisted for the Harper Method. During the war,
women were encouraged to work in war industries and were lured away
from their jobs as shop operators or from studying in training schools.
The hair industry responded by encouraging shops to establish recipro-
cal arrangements with other shops, thereby allowing operators across
the country to work in various locations. Such reciprocity was not a new
concept to the Harper network, but was for the rest of the industry. It
allowed wives to keep working in the field while accompanying their
servicemen husbands (Wynne and Levinger 1995, 23).

While the war brought changes to the personal and work lives of Harper associates, Martha increasingly ignored business and worldly issues. During a yearlong visit, her niece Esther Meeks recalled, her Aunt Mattie was noticeably quiet, socially competent, and gracious, but "no powerhouse." When engaged in conversations, Martha might repeat herself, although she joined them at all social occasions, including dinners at the "club." After at-home meals, Martha gathered the bread crumbs and happily shared them with her feathered friends from her back porch (Meeks 1996a). Her mind often was in another world, and she seemed content with small things.

Martha's gentle spirit remained intact, but by 1944 her behavior became erratic. Robert wanted to refocus the organization, building on its strengths and addressing its weaknesses, yet he had his wife's personal problems to deal with at home. Advertising Manager Jim McGarvey recalled that she was losing her memory (1996). Martha was becoming more needy, afflicted with dementia, and Robert was unable both to lead the business and to attend to Martha. He needed to choose his priority, and he chose Martha.

That decision resulted in the creation of an innovative limited-general partnership agreement. This reorganization enabled Robert to yield the direct business control to Earl Freese, with profits shared between the parties. Technically Robert remained President of the corporation, while Freese continued as the General Manager and took over day-to-day operations. According to Meeks, Freese was selected by Robert even though Robert's brother Ed, Esther's father, strongly advised against hiring him (Meeks 1996a).

The selection of Freese as successor reinforced the male sensibilities and redirection of the firm. He brought a corporate marketing orientation to the unique Harper female organization. Years later, the former head of the Harper School, Hans Neumaier, stated that Freese lacked effective business skills needed for the Harper Method (Neumaier 1995).

Neither the business skills nor the feminist sensitivity of Freese can be adequately evaluated today. What is known is that the Harper leadership had been passed to a man who was used to selling commodities, whose wife did not work, and to whom no direct loyalty between franchisees and franchiser was ever emotionally established. He was also a man with

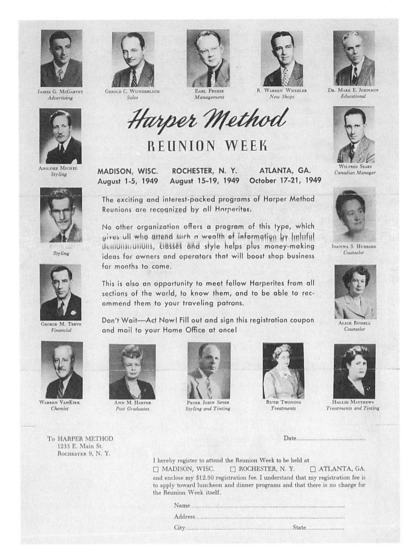

Flyer promoting 1949 Harper Reunion Week includes photos of
management team. Men dominate and two stylists are present.
Courtesy of Betty Wheeler.

a large ego who insisted on being called Dr. Freese immediately after he
received an honorary doctorate from his son's college. His values were
distinctly different from those of Martha, who had refused to change
her name or add a title such as "Madame" to upgrade her image.

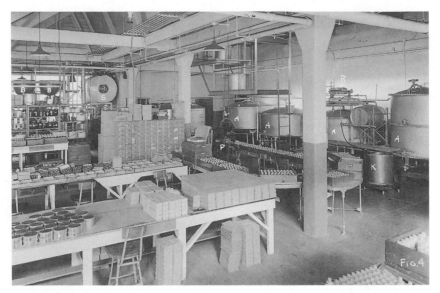

Interior view of Harper "Laboratory." *Courtesy of Betty Wheeler.*

Not surprisingly, Freese changed the way the Harper Method operated. Soon after he took over, Martha's column was eliminated from the
Harper Method Progress and the newsletter was dramatically condensed.
Martha's voice was silenced. The publication no longer shared news of
owners' and operators' trips or the availability of shops for sale. Instead,
the January 1944 newsletter touted a four-color *Harper's Bazaar* advertisement for Harper Method and the front page introduced the new
Harper cold permanent wave solution, calling it Harper's best money
maker in years. The industry had previously embraced such a product
as a profit center in the 1920s.

During this leadership transition, the Harper Method retained a remarkable loyalty among influential Harper patrons and would continue
to do so for decades. This postwar story illustrates the continued devotion and international appeal of the Harper Method.

Paris Shop Owner Louise Weyler Crey, . . . fled from Paris to Vichy France
and waited out [World War II]. Upon [her] return, her Harper Method
shop was found intact . . . , an ad [was] run in the Paris edition of the

New York Herald Tribune and who do you think was the first customer
to enter the shop the following morning. . . . Sir Anthony Eden, then
Foreign Secretary of Britain. (*Romantic Anecdotes of the Harper Method*
n.d., 2)

While the Harper Method maintained this prestigious clientele, home
treatments were expanding. By 1946, the Harper Method and the industry were shaken by the increasing sale of permanent wave kits for
home use. These kits were perceived as a serious and growing threat to
salon business. (Ultimately they simply served to encourage the acceptability of beauty treatments by women.)

Other postwar challenges affected the Harper Method. Servicemen
coming home invaded the job market. With the help of the G.I. Bill,
a number of men chose to train as cosmetologists. As a result, Harper
Schools had a larger number of male trainees and shop owners.

While Freese stumbled to find the right path for the business, other
beauty businesses soared with greater operational efficiencies resulting
from the war and their improved productivity and market responsive-
ness. Elizabeth Arden created a Busy Woman's Beauty Box. Maybelline
pushed eye makeup, suggesting a linkage between powerfully attractive
eyes and getting ahead. Rubinstein launched her Heaven Scent line.

After the war, women were encouraged to leave their war work or
were summarily dismissed to make room for the returning men. The
enthusiasm for female ownership, founded on devotion to Martha and
her Harper principles, gradually evaporated without Martha's leadership
or a charismatic successor to blunt the popular ideal of women belonging at home. Revlon executive Martin Revson, brother of the company's
CEO, ironically used a Thoreau quote to describe women's need for
cosmetics: " 'Most women lead lives of dullness, of quiet desperation.'
The answer for so many lay not in seeking educational and employment
opportunities, as [Betty] Friedan would later argue, but in a 'wonderful
escape' into the fantasy world of feminine beauty" (Peiss 1998, 248).

The Harper business did not grow in proportion to this expanding
market. Overall, beauty shop revenues increased 50 percent from 1948
to 1954 and payrolls increased 45 percent, according to the *Occupa-*

tional Outlook Handbook (1959, 267). Yet, according to an article in the
Denver Post (Dec. 27, 1960), the number of Harper Shops had declined
from its peak of five hundred before the Depression to about three
hundred. Harper Shops still spanned part of the globe, with locations
in the United States, Canada, London, Paris, and Fredrikstad, Norway.

While an aged Martha fed her birds and enjoyed flowers in her garden, Arden and Rubinstein remained vibrant business leaders who often
were more recognized for their personal pursuits. *Notable American
Women* recorded that in 1946 Arden was featured on the cover of *Time*
magazine for her winning horses, not for her successful business (1980,
2). Rubinstein was recognized for her phenomenal jewelry and art collection, her Helena Rubinstein Foundation, and her generous philanthropy to Israel. Yet, until she died at age ninety-five in 1965, Rubinstein
continued to devote the majority of her time to enlarging her business.

By contrast, Martha's loss of her mental faculties prevented her legacy
from continuing with a similar energy and direction. She was removed
from the business and religious institutions she had once valued so deeply.
On April 28, 1941, according to local membership records of the First
Church of Christ, Scientist, an inscription written by Martha's name read
"regularly dismissed." Officially this meant she was no longer a member
of the church. There is no explanation of how or why this occurred,
although this formal withdrawal underscores how much Martha had let
go of the external control she had previously exercised so doggedly.

What is most clear, however, is that until the day she died, Martha
believed she was a Christian Scientist, and certainly two stories from the
1940s suggest she retained her firm belief in Divine Healing. According
to her niece Esther Meeks, Martha fell ill and a doctor, called by Robert,
prescribed some pills. Daily Robert gave Martha the medicine, and
dutifully she took it and reportedly thanked him. When Martha recovered and was removed from the sickroom, Meeks cleaned up and was
shocked to find all of the pills Martha pretended to take—underneath
the bed (Meeks 1997).

From Robert's correspondence, we know that during this decade
Martha broke her arm. He took her to a doctor and insisted that a cast
be put on. Despite Martha's diminished mental awareness, she dragged

herself out of bed and got into a hot bath, where she painfully soaked off her cast.

These stories illustrate both Martha's deep adherence to Christian Science and her husband's increased rejection of her beliefs. He had stopped sending her leather-bound Christian Science books, as he had done during World War I. Instead, he insisted on a medical approach that she firmly rejected. Once Martha was no longer the mentally alert woman she had been, Robert tried to take control. However, Martha resisted, and maintained her fundamental spiritual beliefs.

Robert was Meeks's favorite uncle. She thought of him as debonair and striking with his blue-gray eyes, his sensitivity, and his intelligence. As if he were her Hollywood idol, she hung his photo in her room. Fondly she recalled how he treated her with respect and how much he encouraged her to pursue a career. To further support her modernity, each night he instructed her in the social etiquette of cocktails (Meeks 1996b).

With his wife's increased helplessness, Robert focused on cooking, cleaning, and caring for Martha. To lessen the burden, Martha and he moved to a much smaller home nearby. From a letter to his sister Grace, we gain a glimpse of what Robert faced and how his household responsibilities dominated his world:

> My wife is still quite restricted in her activities, both on account of her arm and also her mental alertness. . . . Sometimes my wife becomes quite forgetful. Nevertheless, she maintains that undying sweetness of disposition and alert sense of humor. Her invalid sister also lives with us, and . . . she is almost entirely a minus quantity.
>
> So you see, I have a good sized job on my hands in looking after these two gals, which involves the management of the house, doing all the kitchen work, minding the garden, doing the shopping, sending out the washing, etc. etc. I sometimes feel it is a little more than I can get done. (R. MacBain 1945a, 1–3)

Robert was intent on keeping Martha's condition a secret, it seems, for her sake and that of the business. The appearance of a March 5, 1946 profile of Martha in the *Christian Science Monitor* "Women Today"

This staged photo of Martha at her desk in 1946
was used by the *Christian Science Monitor* in its
article about her. *Courtesy of Betty Wheeler.*

section illustrates the charade. In the article, titled "Founder of Harper
Method Shops Helps Many Gain Business Independence," Martha was
photographed as if she worked in the office. No mention was made of
Martha's having left Christian Science nor of her diminished mental
capacity (Huntington 1946).

Robert knew the truth, and confided it in a 1947 letter to his sister
Grace. "I must report Martha is still anything but a well lady. More-

over, the doctor tell[s] me we can never hope to see her fully recovered. . . . The lady allows no one to help her or even touch her, except myself. . . . For years, I've been doing all the cooking, housework, cleaning, shopping, etc. . . . I'll have to put little Mattie to bed and ask God to take good care of her while I too try to get a little rest" (R. MacBain 1947, 1–4).

Robert's exhaustion was clear, as was his devotion to Martha. His anger and frustration, however, had grown over the years; he had steadfastly devoted himself to Martha for over twenty-five years. We can only speculate that it was these intense ten years of caretaking that most strained his sense of fairness. In 1943, the first of two codicils to Martha's will was made; it revoked the specific allocation of $16,000 to Martha's sisters and brothers. In April 1947, Martha's will was altered again to ensure that everything went to Robert if he outlived Martha; if he died first, the number of other heirs was reduced. While both codicils removed relatively minor amounts of money from Martha's half-a-million-dollar estate, what was significant about the codicils was that they effectively eliminated the Harper family from Martha's will.

One of the witnesses who signed the 1947 codicil was Jim McGarvey, Harper's Advertising Manager. When asked about the changes and Martha's alertness, McGarvey said, "She was really bad then. I'd say she was totally unaware. I didn't see her sign it . . . I witnessed [the codicil] because the Captain was my boss and he told me to sign it. . . . He signed for her all the time. I wondered how he could get away with it" (McGarvey 1997). Supporting McGarvey's observation about Martha is the fact that she stopped voting after 1945 (Monroe County Board of Elections 1945–1947), a civic duty she had regularly performed since she became a citizen and first voted in 1923.

Robert MacBain must have believed that for all of his devoted service, he deserved the entire estate, and he made sure that no part would be shared with Martha's family if he was alive. The irony is that, above all, Martha wanted family whom she could trust. In the end, her parents, Mrs. Roberts and ultimately, her husband, let her down when it came to honoring financial and family commitments. Unlike her parents, however, Robert did not abandon Martha.

The pretense that Martha remained healthy and alert climaxed in a grand Harper Method finale. Martha's presence, at the age of ninety-one, was the cornerstone of the firm's sixtieth anniversary celebration. Three hundred Harperites gathered in August 1948 to honor her and her business. Twenty-five local and national dignitaries were seated at the banquet's head table, ready to salute the beloved Harper founder. In a melodramatic description of the event to Martha's niece Florence Gilfillan, a Harper Shop owner, Robert recounted the experience without revealing Martha's condition. The event was described as if a coronation took place.

> As the large doors swung open, . . . three words, MARTHA MATILDA HARPER, [were announced]. . . . the great congregation, . . . gave her such an ovation as . . . she never before had. . . .
>
> As [Martha] was [led] to the center of the head table, the audience . . . cheer[ed] until the noise almost became a roar. Having arrived at her place, she stood for a moment waving . . . at the group, smiling and bowing first to the right and then to the left, and throwing kisses to many whom she recognized as the old veterans and pioneers of the Harper Method. Truly, she was the Queen of the occasion, and every eye was fixed upon her during nearly the whole evening's affair. (R. MacBain 1948a, 1)

Robert also identified the significant people who attended and saluted Martha Matilda Harper: "The Mayor of the City had come to deliver a special address acclaiming your Aunty as the foremost woman in the city of Rochester. The president of the Chamber of Commerce announced, to the surprise of most, that . . . [Martha] was the first woman member ever to join the Chamber. There were State Senators and Representatives, Magazine Editors and Writers as well as many other notable people" (R. MacBain 1948a, 1–2).

When a portrait of Martha was presented, the audience learned of its significance: "The painting was done by the famous artist Renold of Beloit, Wisconsin. . . . ultimately this masterpiece will find its way to the National Portrait Gallery in Washington, D.C." (R. MacBain 1948a, 2).

At the sixtieth anniversary dinner in 1948, Martha acknowledges
the cheers from the attending Harperites, public officials, and industry
and community leaders. Her husband, Robert, stands by her side.
Courtesy of Harper Method Progress.

The presentation of the portrait gave the adoring audience another
chance to salute the Harper founder: "At the moment of the unveiling,
the audience was quite taken by surprise.... Most of them without
seeming to realize it, stood with their hands clasped to their bosoms,
almost as if in the attitude of silent prayer" (R. MacBain 1948a, 2).

The keynote speaker articulated the crowd's adoration and placed
Martha's accomplishments into a historical perspective. The speaker,
Florence E. Wall, was a devoted Harper customer, renowned biochem-
ist, fashion consultant, author, New York University scholar, and a fel-
low of the American Institute of Chemists.

That evening, Wall recounted Martha's historic struggles, her pioneering effort, and her current worldwide acclaim. She concluded: "If,
as it has been said, 'We live just as long as there is anyone left that
remembers us,' the latest paradox for Martha Matilda Harper is that

she—this Rebel who became a Pioneer—has progressed a step further, into becoming practically an Immortal before her time" (Wall 1948, 7). If she were alive today, Miss Wall would be shocked to discover that in the annals of history, Harper is no longer remembered.

Yet, as her body and mind diminished, Martha maintained her independent spirit, as she forcefully demonstrated when she rejected her pills and removed her arm cast. Deep down, she knew her soul. One night during the late 1940s, another visiting niece, Fausta Ahrens, Grace's daughter, observed Martha's spirit reassert itself. As usual, Martha had come down dressed for dinner. When they were seated at the dining room table, Robert noticed that Martha had smeared lipstick across her eyebrows. Calmly, but firmly, Robert said, "Now, Mattie, lipstick belongs on your lips, not on your eyebrows. We will have to do something about that." Martha raised herself up in her chair, looked Robert right in the eye, and declared, "If Martha Matilda Harper does it, the world will follow" (Ahrens 1997a). And it has:

• In the year 2000, American franchising, the business vehicle Martha Matilda Harper created, had become the dominant form of retailing and accounted for more than half of all retail sales in America. As of 1998, this business model generated over $800 billion in annual sales.

• In America and Canada, women-owned businesses have become the fastest-growing segment of business ownership. In the decade ending in 1997, the number of women-owned businesses in the United States increased 90 percent, with the aggregate affect that more than 30 percent of all firms in the United States were female-owned. Women-owned business also represented 30 percent of all businesses in Canada and were creating jobs at four times the rate of the top 100 Canadian businesses.

• Today a woman's identity is more often determined by what she does than how she looks. Society, however, still pushes "hope in a jar" rather than Harper's concept of universal inner beauty that simply needs to be released.

• Businesses selling organic, healthful hair and skin products, massages, and skin stimulation processes, like the ones Martha created, are capitalizing on a growing market that generates billions of dollars a year.

- Treatments to prevent baldness support a multibillion-dollar business.
- Customer satisfaction, teamwork, good communication, win-win business strategies, and positive thinking are considered practices of enlightened management. Management gurus like Deming and Moss Kanter are considered brilliant.
- Salons use reclining chairs, based on the design Martha created in 1888, to seat their customers while their hair is being washed.
- The Food and Drug Administration periodically tests the safety of hair dyes.
- Women, once excluded, currently dominate the hair profession in numerical terms. The number of female beauticians, barbers, manicurists in the United States had numbered 3,691, and the number of males in these same positions was 82,157, in 1890. According to the 1990 census, women hairdressers and cosmetologists number 657,433 compared to 66,677 male barbers.
- The number of female hairdressers and barbers in Canada as of 1996 was 68,055; the number of males holding such positions was 15,665.

While Martha's vision for changing the face of American business has come to life, society does not attribute these accomplishments to the determined woman who pioneered them. A look into the mirror of business development reveals no personal image of Martha Matilda Harper, only her business practices. And yet . . . her business, her innovative franchise model, her business principles did operate and alter her own destiny and the destinies of thousands of working-class women who for eighty-four years joined her ranks as loyal operators and owners of the Harper Method of beauty culture.

Epilogue

MARTHA MATILDA HARPER died on August 3, 1950, one month short of her ninety-third birthday. She is buried in Riverside Cemetery in Rochester. Her plot contains a large headstone with a horn of plenty (Martha's trademark) on both the right and the left borders. They pleasantly focus attention on the name *Martha Matilda Harper,* which is boldly inscribed. In smaller letters below are the words *wife of Captain Robert A. MacBain.* Curiously, though the stone has room for another name, there is none.

Robert MacBain died on April 30, 1965, at the age of eighty-three. He is buried next to Martha and has a small in-ground stone that simply bears his name and his military service record.

The combined Harper/MacBain estate totaled over $750,000. All of Martha's money went to her husband. When Robert died, the bulk of his estate went to his alma mater, Simpson College, in Indianola, Iowa. Carillon bells, paid for by Robert and named for Martha, ring daily from the Simpson College chapel, for which Robert provided the major source of funding. In addition, a Pioneer Scholarship Fund was established at Simpson College, and continues to provide needed funding for student education; some MacBain relatives have received such scholarships. Local Rochester charities, including the Susan B. Anthony House, received lesser amounts. MacBain relatives were given token bequests; the Harper relatives received nothing.

The Harper Method Inc. business operated under a variety of owners until 1972. In June 1956, Robert MacBain sold the enterprise to Earl

Freese and Gerald Wunderlich. In the 1960s and 1970s, the new owners made three attempts to sell the business. In 1971, Robert Prentice, then the manager of the Harper manufacturing center in Niagara Falls, Canada, purchased the factory assets along with Harper manufacturing and distribution rights. On March 10, 1972, other Harper Method, Inc., assets were bought by PEJ Beauty Corporation, a wholly owned subsidiary of the Wilfred Academy. At the time, PEJ was one of the largest operators of trade schools in America. According to Philip Jakeway, then President of the Wilfred Academy, he hoped to expand his operation by marketing the Harper products and shops. An agreement was reached whereby Prentice would supply Harper products to Jakeway for U.S. distribution. Jakeway was unsuccessful. Currently, Prentice's business, Niagara Mist Marketing, Ltd., located in St. Catherines, Ontario, retains the formulas for the original Harper products.

The Harper Laboratory, once the headquarters for the Harper empire, still stands with the name *Martha Matilda Harper* clearly etched into its façade. It houses another Rochester business.

The Harper Method Founder's Shop continues to operate in Rochester as the oldest, continuously running beauty shop in the country.

Former Harper customers, operators, and shop owners are still alive, and savor their Harper memories.

WORKS CITED
INDEX

Works Cited

"An Account of the Proceedings of the Susan B. Anthony Trial." 1874. *Rochester Democrat & Chronicle*. Reel 362, no. 250.

Acton, Janice, Penny Goldsmith, and Bonnie Shephard, eds. 1974. *Women at Work: Ontario, 1850–1930*. Toronto: Canadian Women's Educational Press.

Ahrens, Fausta. 1996. Personal interview with author. Eagle Grove, Iowa. May 9.

———. 1997a. Telephone interview with author. Eagle Grove, Iowa. Feb. 2.

———. 1997b. Telephone interview with author. Eagle Grove, Iowa. Aug. 8.

Anderson, Dewey, and Percy E. Davidson. 1940. *Occupations Trends in the U.S.* Stanford, Calif.: Stanford University Press.

Anderson, Mary. 1935. *Inside the Doors of Beauty Shops*. Washington, D.C.: U.S. Government Printing Office.

Anthony, Katherine. 1975. *Susan B. Anthony: Her Personal History and Her Era*. New York: Russell & Russell.

"Baldness." 1933. *Fortune*, 8, no. 1.

Banner, Lois W. 1983. *American Beauty*. New York: Alfred A. Knopf.

The Beautician: The National Magazine of Beauty. 1930–1933. vols. 8–11. Microfilm.

Beeney, Bill. 1973. "Today's Women's Libbers Should Know More About Martha Matilda Harper." *Democrat & Chronicle*. July 19.

Biggart, Nicole Woolsey. 1989. *Charismatic Capitalism: Direct Selling Organizations in America*. Chicago: Univ. of Chicago Press.

The Biographical Record of the City of Rochester and Monroe County, New York. 1902. New York: S. J. Publishing Co.

Braude, Ann. 1989. *Radical Spirits: Spiritualism and Women's Rights in Nineteenth-Century America*. Boston: Beacon Press.

Brownlee, Mary M., and W. Elliot. 1976. *Women in the American Economy: A Documentary History 1675–1929.* New Haven, CT: Yale Univ. Press.

Burke, Barbara. Feb. 1923–Mar. 1934. *Barbara Burke's Beauty Journal.* Microfilm, reels 1–5.

Bushfield, John Harper. 1995. Personal interview with author. Irondequoit, N.Y., Dec. 12.

Cades, Hazel Rawson. 1936. *Jobs for Girls.* New York: Harcourt, Brace.

Candee, Marjorie Dent. 1957. *Current Biography Yearbook.* New York: H. W. Wilson.

Catalogue of Harper Method Training Schools. 1938. Rochester: Harper Method, Inc.

Clune, Henry. 1963. "Seen & Heard." *Democrat & Chronicle.* Sept. 1.

Cornell, Linda. 1966. "Ida M. Tarbell 1857–1944: Muckracker or Historian?" Honors diss., Smith College.

D'Amanda, J. Allis. 1997. Telephone interview with author. Rochester, N.Y., Nov. 17.

De Castelbajac, Kate. 1995. *The Face of the Century: 100 Years of Makeup and Style.* New York: Rizzoli International Publications.

Denver Post. 1960. Dec. 27.

Democrat & Chronicle. 1882. Feb. 2.

Dicke, Thomas S. 1992. *Franchising in America: The Development of a Business Method, 1840–1980.* Chapel Hill: Univ. of North Carolina Press.

Dinse, Frank. 1933. Monroe County Surrogate Court file of Luella Roberts's will. Book 25, 1702.

Dinse, Robert. 1995. Telephone interview with author. Rochester, N.Y. Dec. 7.

Donnelly, Mabel Collins. 1986. *The American Victorian Woman: The Myth and the Reality.* New York: Greenwood Press.

DuBois, Ellen Carol. 1995. "The Radicalism of the Woman's Suffrage Movement: Notes Towards the Reconstruction of Nineteenth-Century Feminism." In *U.S. Women in Struggle: A Feminist Studies Anthology.* Edited by Claire Goldberg Moses and Heidi Hartman. Urbana: Univ. of Illinois Press.

Eddy, Mary Baker. 1934. *Science and Health: With Key to the Scriptures.* Boston: First Church of Christ, Scientist.

Employment Conditions in Beauty Shops: A Study of Four Cities. 1935. Women's Bureau, U.S. Department of Labor. Bulletin 133. Washington, D.C: U.S. Government Printing Office.

Filene, Catherine, ed. 1934. *Careers for Women: New Ideas, New Methods, New Opportunities to Fit a New World*. Boston, Mass.: Houghton Mifflin.

First Church of Christ, Scientist. 1897. Membership records. Rochester, N.Y.

First Church of Christ, Scientist. 1899–1906. Membership records. Rochester, N.Y.

First Church of Christ, Scientist. 1941. Membership records. Rochester, N.Y.

First National Bank Celebration. 1994. Rochester, N.Y.: First National Bank.

Flanders, Maurice. 1933. Monroe County Surrogate Court file of Luella Roberts's will. 1702.

Force, Josephine Sargent. 1933. Monroe County Surrogate Court file of Luella Roberts's will. 1702.

Franchise Opportunities Handbook. 1994. U.S. Dept. of Commerce, Minority Business Development Agency. Washington, D.C.: U.S. Government Printing Office.

Freedman, Estelle. 1995. "Separatism as Strategy: Female Institution Building and American Feminism 1890–1930." In *U.S. Women in Struggle: A Feminist Studies Anthology*. Edited by Claire Goldberg Moses and Heidi Hartman. Urbana: Univ. of Illinois Press.

Freese, Earl. 1956. *To Memorialize Martha Matilda Harper*. Rochester, N.Y.: Harper Method, Inc.

Gamber, Wendy. 1997. *The Female Economy: The Millinery and Dressmaking Trades 1860–1930*. Urbana: Univ. of Illinois Press.

Gammon, Philip. 1933. Monroe County Surrogate Court file of Luella Roberts's will. 1702.

Girvin, Jerry. 1997. Telephone interview with author. Rochester, N.Y. July 8.

Golden Memories. 1938. Rochester, N.Y.: Harper Method, Inc.

Griffin-Cohen, Marjorie. 1988. *Women's Work, Markets and Economy: Development in Nineteenth-Century Ontario*. Toronto: Univ. of Toronto Press.

Haines, Aubrey L. 1977. *The Yellowstone Story: A History of Our First National Park*. Vol. 2. Yellowstone National Park, Wyo.: Yellowstone Library and Museum Association.

Harper, Ann. 1933. Monroe County Surrogate Court file of Luella Roberts's will. 1702.

Harper, Martha Matilda. 1933. Monroe County Surrogate Court file of Luella Roberts's will. 1702.

Harper Method Inc.—Organizational History. Rochester, N.Y.: Harper Method, Inc.

Harper Method Progress. July 1924.

———. Dec. 1925. Vol. 1, no. 8.

———. June–July 1926. Vol. 2, no. 3.

———. July–Aug. 1927. Vol. 3, no. 5.

———. Sept.–Oct. 1927. Vol. 3, no. 6.

———. Sept.–Oct. 1928. Fortieth anniversary issue.

———. March–Apr. 1930.

———. May–June 1930.

———. July–Aug. 1930.

———. Mar.–Apr. 1931, Vol. 8, no. 2.

———. May–June 1931. Vol. 8, no. 3.

———. Nov.–Dec. 1931, Vol. 8, no. 5.

———. July–Aug. 1932. Vol. 9, no. 3.

———. Nov.–Dec. 1932. Vol. 9, no. 3.

———. May 1933, Vol. 10, no. 2.

———. Sept. 1933, Vol. 10, no. 5.

———. March 1935. Vol. 12, no. 2.

———. Oct. 1936, Vol. 13, no. 9.

———. Aug. 1938. Vol. 16, no. 10.

———. Sept. 1938. Vol. 16, no. 11.

———. March 1940. Vol. 17, no. 5.

———. June 1941. Vol. 18, no. 1.

———. Jan. 1944. Vol. 19, no. 1.

———. June 1944, Vol. 19, no. 2.

Harper Method Textbook. 1926. Rochester, N.Y.: Martha Matilda Harper, Inc.

Hawley Records. Oakville, Ont.: Oakville Historical Society.

Hersa, Elig 1988. *The Beauty Queens.* R Marts Production. Chicago: Public Media Release. Video.

Hewitt, Nancy A. 1984. *Women's Activism and Social Change: Rochester, New York, 1822–1872.* Ithaca, N.Y.: Cornell Univ. Press.

———. 1995. "Feminist Friends: Agrarian Quakers and the Emergence of Women's Rights in America." In *U.S. Women in Struggle: A Feminist Studies Anthology.* Edited by Claire Goldberg Moses, and Heidi Hartman. Urbana: Univ. of Illinois Press.

Hickey, Berta. 1996. Personal interview with author. Burnt River, Ont. June· 13.

Holbrook, Stewart H. 1953. *The Age of the Moguls.* Garden City, N.Y.: Doubleday.

Holahan, Elizabeth. 1994. Personal interview with author. June 21. Rochester, N.Y.

Hoskinson, Jack, and Robert Hoskinson. 1996. Personal interview with author. May 6, Indianola, Iowa.

Hoskinson, Lillian. 1923. Letter to brother Allen. July.

Howell, Christine Moore. 1936. *Beauty Culture and Care of Hair.* New Brunswick, N.J.: Hill Publishing Co.

Howk, Cynthia. 1996. Memo for file of Landmark Society of Western New York. Rochester. Feb. 8.

Huntington, Lucille. 1946. "Founder of Harper Method Shops Helps Many Gain Business Independence." *The Christian Science Monitor,* "Women To-day" section. Mar. 5.

Jensen, Oliver, ed. 1967. *The Nineties.* New York: American Heritage.

Jones, Alpha E. 1996. Obituary. *State Journal Register* (Springfield, Ill.). Aug. 12.

Jones, Thomas B. 1968. *How the Negro Can Start His Own Business: A Guide to Owning and Operating a Franchised Business.* Brooklyn, N.Y.: Albert Press.

Kelly, Arthur, ed. 1934. *The Book of the Rochester Centennial.* Rochester, N.Y.: Rochester Centennial, Inc.

Kessler-Harris, Alice. 1981. *Women Have Always Worked: A Historical Overview.* Old Westbury, N.Y.: Feminist Press.

Knapp, Sally. 1997. Personal interview with author. Baltimore. Jan. 24.

Korf, Frederick. 1923. *Art and Fundamentals of Hairdressing.* New York: Wilfred Academy of Hair & Beauty Culture.

LaLonde, Flora. 1933. Monroe County Surrogate Court file of Luella Roberts's will. Book 25, 1702.

Leetooze, Sherrel Branton. 1988. *From the Oak Plain to the Lakefront: A Brief History of Clarke Township.* Bowmanville, Ont.: Lynn Michael-John Associates.

Leve, Austin. 1995. Telephone interview with author. Rochester, N.Y. Dec. 6.

Livesay, Harold C. 1975. *Andrew Carnegie and the Rise of Big Business.* Boston: Little, Brown.

Maas, Virginia H. 1979. "Martha Harper and Her Magic Formula." *Hairstylist* (Apr.–May).

MacBain, Elspet. 1912. Letter to her son Eddie. Nodaway, Iowa. June 30.

MacBain, Robert. n.d. Family history of the MacBains.

———. 1910. Letter to the Greenfield relations. Indianola, Iowa. June 12.

————. 1918. Letter to mother, Elspet MacBain. France. Dec. 28.

————. 1921. Letter to mother, Elspet MacBain. Rochester, N.Y. Oct.

————. 1921. Letter to mother, Elspet MacBain. Rochester, N.Y. Dec.

————. 1933. Monroe County Surrogate Court file of Luella Roberts's will. Book 25, 1702.

————. 1943. Letter to sister Grace Wycoff. Rochester, N.Y. Dec. 13.

————. 1945a. Letter to sister Grace Wycoff. Rochester, N.Y. July 11.

————. 1945b. "Miss Harper's Career." Rochester, N.Y. Sept. 12.

————. 1947. Letter to sister Grace Wycoff. Rochester, N.Y. Sept. 30.

————. 1948a. Letter to niece Florence Gilfillan. Rochester, N.Y. Sept. 1.

————. 1948b. Letter to Mrs. Hazel C. Matthews. Dec. 6.

————. 1953. Letter to sister Grace Wycoff. Rochester, N.Y. Sept. 29.

————. 1954. Letter to sister Grace Wycoff. Rochester, N.Y. June 25.

————. 1957. Letter to Lois and Ed MacBain. Rochester, N.Y. Feb. 5.

————. 1964. Letter to Lois MacBain. Rochester, N.Y. Sept. 4.

MacMurchy, Marjory. 1914. "Martha Matilda Harper, a Woman Who Has Succeeded." *The Toronto*. June 6.

The Madam C. J. Walker Beauty Manual: A Thorough Treatise Covering All Branches of Beauty Culture. n.d. Indianapolis: The Madam C. J. Walker Manufacturing Co.

Matthews, Hazel C. 1953. *Oakville and the Sixteen: The History of an Ontario Port*. 3rd ed. Toronto: Univ. of Toronto Press.

McGarvey, Jim. 1996. Personal interview with author. Rochester, N.Y. July 24.

————. 1997. Personal interview with author. Rochester, N.Y. Mar. 6.

McKelvey, Blake. 1941. "Economic Stages in the Growth of Rochester." *Rochester History*, 3, no. 4 (Oct.).

————. 1980. *A Panoramic History of Rochester and Monroe County New York*. Woodland Hills, Calif.: Windsor Publications.

————. 1993. *Rochester on the Genesee: The Growth of a City*. Syracuse: Syracuse Univ. Press.

Meeks, Esther. 1996a. Personal interview with author. Terre Haute, Ind. May 2.

————.1996b. Phone interview with author. Terre Haute, Ind. Sept. 8.

————.1996c. Phone interview with author. Terre Haute, Ind. Oct. 13.

————.1997. Phone interview with author. Terre Haute, Ind. Oct. 28.

Merrill, Arch. 1986. *Rochester Sketchbook*. Interlaken, N.Y.: Empire State Books.

Meyerowitz, Joanne J. 1988. *Women Adrift: Independent Wage Earners—Chicago, 1880–1930*. Chicago: Univ. of Chicago Press.

"Mr. Berry's Comments on Captain MacBain." 1966. Simpson College Board Minutes, attachment 1. Indianola, Iowa. May 28.

Monroe County Board of Elections. 1923–1947. Voting records. Rochester, N.Y.

"National Business Hall of Fame, The." 1992. *Fortune*. March 13.

Neumaier, Hans. 1995. Personal interview with author. Henrietta, N.Y. Nov. 12.

Notable American Women. 1980. Vol. 4. Edited by Barbara Sicherman and Carol Hurd Green. Cambridge, Mass.: Harvard Univ. Press.

Oakville (Ont.) Historical Society Newsletter. 1996. Dec.

Obituary Compilation of Martha Matilda Harper. 1950. Rochester, N.Y.: The Harper Method, Inc.

O'Higgins, Patrick. 1971. *Madame: An Intimate Biography of Helena Rubinstein*. New York: Viking Press.

Occupational Outlook Handbook. 1959. U.S. Department of Labor, Bureau of Labor Statistics. Bulletin 1255. Washington, D.C.: U.S. Government Printing Office.

O'Leary, Catherine Harper. 1996a. Personal interview with author. Lindsay, Ont. June 14.

———. 1996b. Personal interview with author. Lindsay, Ont. Oct. 29.

Orono Star. 1857. Apr. 9.

Pancoast, Helen. 1998. Letter to author. Miami, Fla. Feb. 9.

Peel, Robert. 1988. *Health and Medicine in the Christian Science Tradition: Principles, Practice and Challenge*. New York: Crossroads.

Peiss, Kathy. 1990. "Making Faces: The Cosmetics Industry and the Cultural Construction of Gender, 1890–1930." *Genders*, 7 (Mar.).

———. 1998. *Hope in a Jar*. New York: Henry Holt.

"Potpourri." 1930. *Fortune*, 11, no. 2 (Aug.).

Purdy, Janet Levaux. 1995. "Leaders and Success: Entrepreneur Helena Rubinstein. She Merged a Strong Business Sense with an Eye for Art." *Investors Business Daily*. Feb. 1.

Rayne, Martha Louise. 1884. *What Can a Woman Do—Her Position in the Business and Literary World*. Detroit: F. B. Dickerson.

Re Roberts' Will. 1935. 283 N.Y.S. Nov. 13.

Reed, Jane. 1996. Phone interview with author. Miami, Fla. Nov. 17.

—. 1997. Personal interview with author. Miami, Fla. Jan. 24.

Riker, Dorothy. 1995. Personal interview with author. Penfield, N.Y. Nov. 6.

Roberts, Elizabeth. 1995. *Women's Work 1840–1940*. Cambridge, Mass.: Cambridge Univ. Press.

Rochester Commerce. 1954. "Rochester Pioneers: Martha Matilda Harper." 41, no. 5 (May).

———. 1963. "Seventy Five Years of Harper Method in Rochester." 50, no. 7 (Aug.).

Roemer, Lillian. 1997. Personal interview with author. Rochester, N.Y. July 7.

Romantic Anecdotes of the Harper Method. n.d. Rochester, N.Y.: Harper Method, Inc.

Rosenberg-Naparsteck, Ruth. 1989. "Two Centuries of Industry and Trade in Rochester." *Rochester History,* 51, no. 4 (Fall).

Ross, Ishbel. 1962. *Grace Coolidge and Her Era: The Story of a President's Wife.* New York: Dodd, Mead.

———. 1963. *Crusades and Crinolines: The Life and Times of Ellen Curtis Demorest and William Jennings Demorest.* New York: Harper & Row.

Rubenstein, Alice. 1997a. Personal correspondence with author. Pittsford, N.Y. Jan. 19.

———. 1997b. Personal interview with author. Rochester, N.Y. Apr. 11.

———. 1997c. Personal interview with author. Rochester, N.Y. Oct. 27.

Sailer, Centa. 1995. Personal interview with author. Rochester, N.Y. Dec. 11.

Schmid, Helen, and Sid Schmid. 1982. *Out of the Mists: A History of Clarke Township.* 2nd ed. Oshawa, Ont.: Maracle Press.

The Scientific Care of the Hair and Scalp. 1932. Rochester, N.Y. Martha Matilda Harper.

Shaffer, Lee E. 1993. Obituary. *Reading (Pa.) Eagle.* Mar. 7.

Simpson College. 1954. Biography of Robert MacBain. Indianola, Iowa.

Smith, Frank. 1997. Letter to author. Boston. Jan. 8.

Spelman, Edwin. 1997. Phone interview with author. Rochester, N.Y. July 8.

———. *Spelman's Notebook.* n.d. Charlotte, N.Y. Charlotte Lighthouse Society.

Squair, John. 1927. *The Township of Darlington and Clarke: Including Bomanville and Newcastle.* Toronto: Univ. of Toronto Press.

Thure, Karen. 1976. "Martha Harper Pioneered in the Hair Business." *Smithsonian.* Sept.

Van Alstyne, Eunice. 1996a. Telephone interview with author. Webster, N.Y. Jan. 9.

———. 1996b. Personal interview with author. Webster, N.Y. Jan. 24.

Wall, Florence E. 1948. *Martha M. Harper: Pioneer Career Woman.* 1948. Rochester, N.Y.: Harper Method Inc.

Wentworth, Blanche. 1933. Monroe County Surrogate Court file of Luella Roberts's will. 1702.

Wheeler, Betty. 1996. Personal interview with author. Viola, Wis. May 3.

Willard, Frances. 1897. *Occupations for Women.* New York: The Success Co.

Willoughby, Mary. 1933. Monroe County Surrogate Court file of Luella Roberts's will. Book 25, 1702.

"Women in Business III." 1935. *Fortune,* 12, no. 3.

Wynne, Janet Ruegg, and Ivan D. Levinger. 1995. *NCA's Diamond Jubilee Year.* Korea: National Cosmetology Association.

Xerox Historical Museum. n.d. *Midtown Plaza.* Rochester, N.Y.: The Museum.

Zinn, Howard, 1995. *A People's History of the United States 1492–Present.* New York: Harper Perennial.

Index